Fort Gaines, Georgia

A Military History

Dale Cox & Rachael Conrad

2016

ISBN: 978-0692802250

Volume 2 in the Forts of the Forgotten Frontier Series

Visit the author online at:

www.exploresouthernhistory.com

Old Kitchen Books
An Old Kitchen Media Company
4523 Oak Grove Road
Bascom, Florida 32423

"Think not that I am come to send peace on earth:
I came not to send peace, but a sword."
Matthew 10:34

This book is respectfully dedicated to the memory of Elizabeth Dill.

Table of Contents

1.
In the wake of Fort Jackson / 1

2.
Establishment of Fort Gaines / 9

3.
Raiders at Fort Gaines / 21

4.
Fort Scott and the "Negro Fort" / 33

5.
The Winter of 1816-1817 / 47

6.
Tensions on the Frontier / 63

7.
The First Seminole War / 73

8.
Warrior Executions at Fort Gaines / 89

9.
The Remarkable Story of Elizabeth Dill / 97

10.
The Forts on the Bluff / 127

Photographs / 137

References / 149

Maps

1.
Southwest Georgia / 12

2.
Fort Gaines, 1816 / 18

Introduction

Fort Gaines was a U.S. military post on the lower Chattahoochee River in Georgia. Built in 1816 by soldiers of the 4th Infantry Regiment, it served a variety of roles during its five-year history. Lt. Col. Duncan Lamont Clinch first used it as a jumping off point for his operations against the large maroon community at Prospect Bluff, Florida. The site of the "Negro Fort" that American forces destroyed is now a national historic landmark and Fort Gaines played an important role in that history of national significance.

The fort then served as the southernmost and westernmost defensive bastion on Georgia's frontier with the Creek Nation. Its garrison was for a time the only defensive barrier that stood between Native American warriors outraged over the massive land cession forced upon them at the Treaty of Fort Jackson and the American settlers who were already crowding to occupy their lands. Fort Gaines was an important supply depot during the First Seminole War of 1817-1818 and was the base for the operations of Brig. Gen. William McIntosh's Creek Brigade during that conflict.

It remained a garrisoned U.S. military post until 1821, but was occupied again by Georgia Militia in 1836 and Confederate forces in 1863-1865. Each of these groups built new fortifications on the site, extending the history of Fort Gaines into new eras of time.

This book follows the history of this unique and important fort through eyewitness accounts, military reports and contemporary news items. Regular readers of my books will recognize some of this material from my earlier work *Fort Scott, Fort Hughes & Camp Recovery*. The histories of these sites are closely linked with that of Fort Gaines, yet each place has an individual story that is significant and worthy of extended exploration.

I am grateful to many people and institutions for their assistance in the writing and publication of this volume. Thank you especially to the staffs at the National Archives, Library of Congress, National Archives of Great Britain, Georgia State Archives, Florida State Archives, Alabama State Archives and other governmental repositories. Numerous libraries and universities provided access to their collections but I am especially indebted to Dean DeBolt at the University of West

Florida's West Florida History Center in Pensacola for access to their wealth of documentation on the War of 1812 and First Seminole War.

Thanks must also be extended to Rhonda Kimbrough and Andrea Repp of the U.S. Forest Service, Christopher Kimball, Joe Knetsch, John and Mary Lou Missall of the Seminole War Foundation, Nancy White, the City of Chattahoochee and Chattahoochee Main Street, Sue Tindel, Robert Earl Standland, Pearl Cox, William Cox, Alan Cox, the late E.W. Carswell, Brian Mabelitini, Gregg Harding, Mike Thomin of the Florida Public Archaeology Network, the U.S. Army Corps of Engineers, Mike Bunn of Historic Blakeley State Park, Clayton Penhallegon of the Historic Chattahoochee Commission and especially the people of Fort Gaines, Georgia.

Rachael Conrad of Old Kitchen Media provided so much assistance in the research and writing of this book that I am listing her as the coauthor.

May God bless and keep all of you.

Dale Cox
October 27, 2016

Fort Gaines, Georgia

A Military History

Dale Cox & Rachael Conrad

CHAPTER ONE

In the wake of Fort Jackson

The establishment of Fort Gaines on the Chattahoochee River was a direct result of the Creek War of 1813-1814 and the related signing of the Treaty of Fort Jackson on August 9, 1814. The treaty brought the Creek War to a close, but imposed upon the nation a cession of 23,000,000 acres along the border of Spanish Florida in what is now Southwest Georgia and South Alabama. The agreement was the brainchild of Major General Andrew Jackson, who had defeated the nativist or Red Stick branch of the Creeks at the Battle of Horseshoe Bend on March 27, 1814. Jackson considered the cession to be a fair indemnification to the United States for the expenses that it incurred during the war, but to the Creeks it was a national outrage that penalized friend and foe alike. The new "public lands" completely separated the dwindling territory of the Creeks from the Gulf Coast and their former Spanish benefactors in Florida.

From a point on the Coosa River at the "Great Falls," present-day Wetumpka, Alabama the northern boundary of the Fort Jackson cession crossed overland to the nearby Tallapoosa River which it then followed upstream for a short distance. From a point ten miles above the mouth of the

Tallapoosa, the line ran east in "a direct line to the mouth of Summochico creek, which empties into the Chatahouchie river on the east side thereof below the Eufaulau town, thence east from a true meridian line to a point which shall intersect the line now dividing the lands claimed by the said Creek nation from those claimed and owned by the state of Georgia."[1]

The Treaty of Fort Jackson was signed by 31 Creek leaders, all but one of whom had sided with the United States during the war. It effectively ended the conflict, but also inspired new animosity among thousands of Native Americans.

The cession was particularly shocking to Lower Creeks who lived below the line in Southwest Georgia and Southeast Alabama. Most of their towns had stayed out of the war, but they had been given no part in the treaty negotiations. Now they were being told that they must give up the lands of their ancestors and move up to within the new limits established for their nation, lands where they had neither homes nor fields. Similarly outraged by news of the treaty were the thousands of Red Stick warriors who had fled into Spanish Florida after the Battle of Horseshoe Bend. Now supported by the British, they formed an alliance with the Miccosukee and Alachua Seminoles and began an accelerating series of small raids into Georgia and Alabama. The latter state was then part of the Mississippi Territory.

The situation achieved critical mass when U.S. surveyors tried to to mark the limits of the new cession. Anger surged, although the Creeks were so exhausted from war and their resources so depleted from the cataclysmic destruction nation. Most could do little more than oppose the survey with words, but a few showed that their willingness to fight had not been completely extinguished:

> The Indians, however, still adhere to their resolution not to permit their interpreters and hunters to go upon the line. This alone, considering the Indian Character, can not but be viewed as a strong indication of dissatisfaction, if not of hostility. But we have lately received unquestionable information of an outrage which leaves no doubt that a spirit of hostility exists in a part of the nation. A Colonel

> Powell, a Captain Daniel Johnston, and another person from the neighborhood of Fort Stoddert, were some 10 or 12 days ago fired on by a party of Indians near Fort Claiborne. Powell only escaped, three balls having passed through his clothes.[2]

The author of the above was Brevet Major General Edmund P. Gaines, a figure well known in the Mississippi Territory for his role in the 1807 arrest of former vice president Aaron Burr. He had served on the Niagara frontier during the War of 1812, gaining national acclaim during the heroic defense of Fort Erie against a larger British army. Gaines had been badly wounded in that engagement. By January of 1816 he had been placed in command of the Eastern Division of Major General Andrew Jackson's Military Department of the South. General Gaines, like the Tennessee frontiersman David Crockett, would later oppose Jackson's policy of Indian Removal.

Gaines investigated reports of the attack on Powell's party and soon began to refer to the incident as the "Johnson & McGaskey murders," a reference to the men who had lost their lives. The 1816 Census of Baldwin County, Alabama, lists both Daniel Johnson and John McGaskey as residents of the seven-year-old county. Their presence so early on a frontier then best known as the site of the 1813 Creek attack on Fort Mims indicates that they were probably trying to improve their fortunes by seeking good lands on the leading edge of American expansion. Contrary to the rules published by the U.S. military, they lost their lives by venturing into a region still frequented by Savannah Jack and other Red Stick chiefs and warriors.[3]

The murders of Johnson and McGaskey brought the running of the survey to a temporary halt. General Gaines ordered Lt. Col. Duncan Lamont Clinch to march his battalion of the 4th U.S. Infantry Regiment to take up a line of march from Fort Hawkins in central Georgia to Fort Mitchell on the Chattahoochee River. The latter post was in the Creek Nation and had been established by General John Floyd's army of Georgia militia during the Creek War. Although it was established as a base for land operations against Red Stick groups south of the Tallapoosa River, Fort Mitchell also had the advantage of being near the head of navigation on the Chattahoochee. The general planned for Clinch's men to build flatboats that they would use to descend the river to the mouth of Cemochechobee Creek, the point where the cession line struck the Chatahoochee River. Everything below that point was now the land of the United States.[4]

Gaines' plan was evident. Col. Clinch would establish a new post at the Cemochechobee to establish an American presence in the new public lands. This would be augmented by a second new fort to be built on or near the Conecuh River north of Pensacola. Combined with existing posts such as Fort Mitchell, Fort Claiborne, Fort Jackson, Fort Williams and Fort Strother, these forts would allow U.S. troops to virtually surround the surviving lands of the Creek Nation.

The general also had his eye on another target, the so-called "Negro Fort" at Prospect Bluff on the Apalachicola River. This powerful work had been built by British troops under Lt. Col. Edward Nicolls in 1814-1815. Downstream from Fort Mitchell and the proposed new post at the mouth of Cemochechobee Creek, it was held by a large force of maroons or runaway slaves. Most of these individuals were from Spanish Florida and had enlisted in Nicolls' battalion of British colonial marines. Gaines and others feared that the fort was a beacon to the slaves that worked the plantations in Georgia, the Carolinas and the Mississippi Territory. The "Underground Railroad" then ran south into Spanish Florida.

Slaveholders in the United States, Spanish Florida and the Creek Nation feared the influence of the well-armed maroons at Prospect Bluff. All three nations were developing plans for dealing with the perceived threat of the "Negro Fort" and Gaines clearly had a military campaign against the fort in mind when he told Andrew Jackson that the boats being built to carry Clinch's battalion to the Cemochechobee would also prove valuable should it become "necessary to extend our operations lower down the river. There was no way that Jackson would not recognize the hint, but Gaines left no doubt when he concluded his report with the latest intelligence about the maroon establishment on the Apalachicola.[5]

Attacks by Red Sticks and the perceived threat from the fort on the Apalachicola were not the only issues facing the U.S. Army on the frontier.

Settlers were trying to squat on the new "public lands" and offered a serious threat to government plans to sell the land. On February 20, two days after his report on the Johnson and McGaskey murders, General Gaines published a broadside from the War Department that bluntly told potential settlers to stay off the treaty lands. Anyone found squatting there after March 10, 1816, would be removed by force and suffered to witness the destruction of their homes and property.[6]

The warning also extended to those who might be so foolhardy as to trespass on the remaining lands of the Creek Indians:

> Intrusion upon the lands of the friendly Indian tribes, is not only a violation of the laws, but in direct opposition to the policy of the government towards its savage neighbors. Upon application of any Indian agent stating that intrusions of this nature have been committed, and are continued, the President requires that they shall be equally removed, and their habitations and improvements destroyed by military force, and that every attempt to return shall be repressed in the same manner.[7]

Communications of the time were slow but it did not take long for news of the troubling situation to reach the people of Georgia. The *Augusta Chronicle* reported on March 1st that Gaines had ordered U.S. troops to the frontier. A more detailed article followed three days later with news on Creek opposition to the running of the cession lines:

> *Creek Nation.* – A serious misunderstanding, which threatens the peace and tranquility of our frontiers, still exists between our commissioners for running the new boundary line and the chiefs of that confederacy. A determined opposition has been made to their farther progress, and we understand they have suspended their operations until a sufficient military force arrives to protect them from indignity and injury. General Gaines, who is now in the nation, has ordered all the disposable military

> force of the United States, now at Fort Hawkins, among which is a company of light artillery, to march immediately to Fort Mitchell. This precautionary measure we hope will have its desired effect, and that the misguided savage will avert that destruction, which threatens the extinction of his nation.[8]

The soldiers themselves believed that they were going to war. One officer wrote to a friend in Richmond, Virginia, on March 20th that "we are going to have a Creek war to a certainty." The writer noted that he was taking eight companies of infantry and one of artillery to the Creek Nation where Gen. Gaines was determined to run the line "PEACEABLY IF HE CAN, FORCIBLY IF HE MUST." The words were in the upper case in the original.[9]

Gaines reported to Jackson that day on the movement of Clinch's battalion. The soldiers had crossed the Flint River on the 16th, he noted, and should be either at or near Fort Mitchell. Gaines was less convinced than the anonymous letter writer quoted by the *Augusta Chronical* that war was imminent, but clearly indicated that he was more than willing to spark a new conflict. After telling Jackson. After telling Jackson that a military escort would allow the surveyors to complete their work in two weeks, he suggested to Jackson the establishment of yet another new post even lower down the Chattahoochee. Such a fort, he wrote, could be used as a base for the destruction of the fort at Prospect Bluff:

> Should a post be established, its supplies, I am persuaded may be derived more conveniently and more economically from Mobile or New Orleans than any other source. If such an intercourse could be opened down the Appalachacola, it would enable us to keep an eye upon the Seminoles and the Negro Fort. This Negro establishment is, (I think justly,) considered as likely to produce much evil, among the blacks of Georgia & the eastern part of the Mississippi Territory. Will you permit me to break it up?[10]

Gaines was confident of Jackson's backing and began to put his plan into motion. Setting out on horseback he reached Fort Mitchell on March

21, 1816. There he found Lt. Col. Clinch and his men building seven large flatboats. Orders were sent to Major David E. Twiggs of the 7th Infantry, then at Fort Montgomery near the site of Fort Mims, instructing him to build a new fort on the Conecuh River at or just above the Florida line. The post would prove difficult to establish, but was in place on the high bluffs overlooking Murder Creek at what is now East Brewton, Alabama, by that summer. Then, without waiting for General Jackson's response to the report detailing his plan, Gaines led Clinch's force down the Chattahoochee River. The flatboats left Fort Mitchell on March 31.[11]

---

[1] Treaty of Fort Jackson, August 9, 1814.
[2] Maj. Gen. Edmund P. Gaines to Maj. Gen. Andrew Jackson, February 20, 1816, Andrew Jackson Papers, Library of Congress.
[3] Dixie May Jones and Mary Elizabeth Scott, Citizens of Baldwin County, Mississippi Territory, in 1816 as enumerated in *Inhabitants of Alabama in 1816*, Broken Arrow Chapter, Daughters of the American Revolution, 1955.
[4] Gaines to Jackson, February 20, 1816.
[5] *Ibid.*
[6] Notice from Headquarters of Maj. Gen. Edmund P. Gaines, February 22, 1816, Spooner's Vermont Journal, April 15, 1816, p. 3.
[7] Orders of Hon. William Crawford, Secretary of War, included in Notice from Headquarters of Maj. Gen. Edmund P. Gaines, February 22, 1816, *Ibid.*
[8] *Augusta Chronicle*, March 6,1816.
[9] *Baltimore Patriot*, March 20, 1816, citing a letter from an officer to a friend in Richmond probably from February.
[10] Maj. Gen. Edmund P. Gaines to Maj. Gen. Andrew Jackson, March 20, 1816, Andrew Jackson papers, Library of Congress.
[11] Maj. Gen. Edmund P. Gaines to Maj. Gen. Andrew Jackson, April 18, 1816, Andrew Jackson papers, 1775-1874, Library of Congress.

CHAPTER TWO

Establishment of Fort Gaines

The seven flatboats under General Gaines and Lt. Col. Clinch reached the mouth of Cemochechobee Creek on April 2, 1816. The two officers conducted a brief survey of the surrounding area but the ideal location for their new fort was readily evident. An impressive bluff rises above the east bank of the Chattahoochee River just south of its confluence with the Cemochechobee. Its crest provides a remarkable view of the river valley while to the west and north can be seen miles of the cession lands as well as the southern edge of the treaty-reduced Creek Nation.[1]

Clinch had no real combat experience, but Gaines had defended fortified positions in battle and quickly recognized the strategic value of the bluff. The height was certainly perfect for watching the river and surrounding countryside, while the steep three-sided nature of the escarpment made it very defensible. Orders were issued and the sounds of axes soon rang out as the soldiers of the 4th Infantry began to build the new fort that they would name for their general:

> ...The Lt. Colonel has commenced a small work, consisting of a square picketing and two block houses, to

> be defended by one company. The site is strong, handsome and apparently healthy. It is upon the left bank of the river on a hill or bluff 133 feet, nearly perpendicular from the edge of the water.[2]

Fort Gaines was not a large structure. The general had described it as "small" and noted that it could be defended by one company. A fort of similar design was built the following year on the Flint River with exterior walls that measured 90 feet on each side. That structure – Fort Hughes at present-day Bainbridge – was also designed to be defended by a single company. Each of the forts had two blockhouses. Located diagonally across the parade ground from each other, these log buildings provided a way for the muskets of the garrisons to sweep the stockade walls in the event of an attack. The blockhouses at Fort Gaines were square and two stories tall. The second level was larger than the first and featured an overhang on all four sides. If of the same dimensions as those built at Fort Hughes, the blockhouses of Fort Gaines measured 20 by 20 feet on the lower level and 24 by 24 feet on the upper. Since the fort was built to watch over the southern border of the Creek Nation at the point where the Fort Jackson treaty line crossed the Chattahoochee River, it is logical to assume that one of the two blockhouses was located on its northwest corner. By default, then, the other would have been on the southwest angle.[3]

The first survey of District 5 of the original Early County, Georgia, shows Fort Gaines to have been located at about the center of the southern half of fractional Land Lot 395. As the plat was prepared by surveyor Joel Walker in 1819 when the original fort was still occupied, it is undoubtedly accurate and shows the post to have been located near the northern end of the river face of the bluff. A comparison of the 1819 map with modern city maps indicates that the stockade probably stood between the edge of the bluff and Old Pioneer Cemetery. The historic cemetery, in fact, may have originated as the original burial ground of the post as it is known to have been in use prior to 1830. This would place the site of the fort somewhere near the western end of Carroll Street and its intersection with Jackson Street in modern Fort Gaines, probably between Jackson and Bluff Streets and south of Commerce Street. While a portion of the bluff was dug away during the construction of the modern bridge over the Chattahoochee River, it appears likely that most if not all of the original fort site survives.[4]

The name "Fort Gaines" first appeared in military documents on April 5, 1816. Brevet Maj. Enos Cuter used the new designation when he submitted Inspection Returns for the seven companies present to the office of the Adjutant and Inspector General. The cover letter indicates that the units were then stationed at "Fort Gaines, Chattohuche R."[5]

Because the stockade was designed to house only one company, most of Clinch's men camped on the newly cleared land surrounding it. The presence of so many soldiers concerned the residents of nearby Creek villages. To better explain the impact of the Treaty of Fort Jackson on these communities, Gaines and Clinch called for a council with the chiefs and leading men. The Big Warrior of the Upper Creeks and Little Prince of the Lower Creeks were in attendance, as was the war chief William McIntosh of Coweta:

> …I explained to the Indians settled near Summochichoba the object of our movement – to complete the line according to the Treaty, and lay off the land, that our people may buy and settle it – That I brought the pipe of peace for our friends – and for our enemies the cannon & bayonet. They replied that they were too poor and too weak to oppose us, and therefore had determined to sit still and hold down their heads.[6]

The passive response of the chiefs reflected their recognition of the fact that they could not hope to oppose the United States. Whether they approved of the military mission or not, they had neither the arms nor the warriors to do anything about it. The council convinced Gaines that the running of the cession line would now go smoothly and he left for Camp Montgomery on the Alabama River on April 7, 1816. His total residence at the post that now bore his name had lasted only five days.

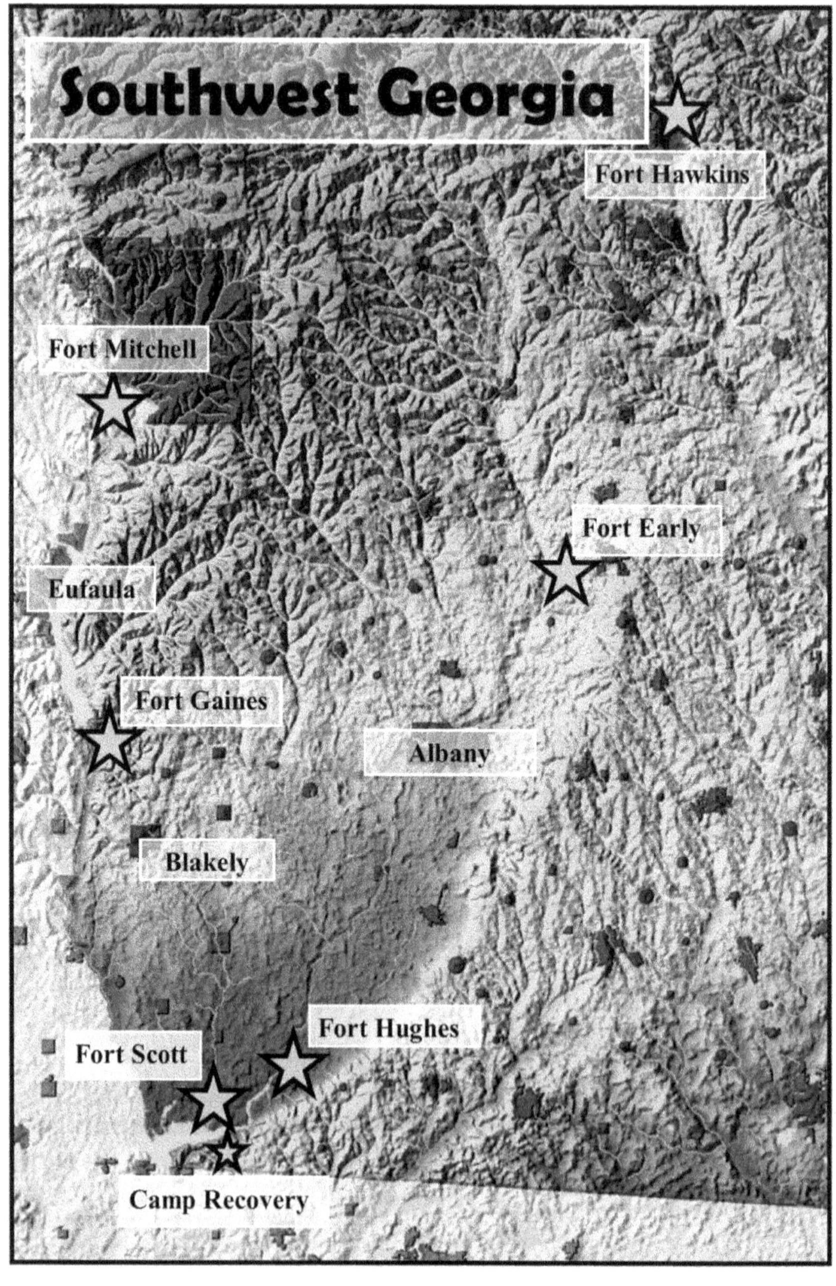
Southwest Georgia
Fort Hawkins
Fort Mitchell
Fort Early
Eufaula
Fort Gaines
Albany
Blakely
Fort Hughes
Fort Scott
Camp Recovery

The council convened by Gaines and Clinch gave one officer from the 4th Infantry an intimate view of several of the leading figures in the Creek Nation:

> ...I had the opportunity of seeing the Indians in council, where the Big Warrior and Little Prince were both present. You no doubt will recollect that the Big Warrior was friendly to us during the late war. Let me tell you he does not conceal is disapprobation to our running the boundary line. However he received us courteously – not so the Little Prince, who showed us no mark of attention. The Big Warrior is the largest Indian known to us. He is dignified in his demeanor, affable and inviting in his manners; his enemies accuse him of cowardice, but I presume his inactivity of late years is to be ascribed to old age and an unwieldy person. The countenance of the Little Prince indicates him to be fierce and cruel, and I am told it does not belie him. It is perhaps well for the United States, that he is now old and bigoted. There is also another very important personage in the nation – I mean the famous M'Intosh – the same to whom Congress gave a sword for services, &c. and to whom we are more indebted for our victories over the Indians in the late war than some persons would be willing to admit. He is a half breed, and but chief of a town. His figure would rival the Apollo, and such an air of majesty I never beheld. His every motion displays all that grace, dignity and elegance which you would imagine the Grecian model, when animated, to possess.[7]

The Creeks did not offer armed resistance to the establishment of Fort Gaines, but another problem soon arose that threatened the very existence of the post. The U.S. Army contracted with suppliers who were responsible for delivering provisions and other necessities to the nation's military installations. The contractor for Georgia, however, refused to supply Fort

Gaines due to its isolated and dangerous location. He claimed that his contract required him to deliver only to populated areas. General Gaines referred the matter to the War Department while also urging General Jackson to push a supply to the fort by way of the Apalachicola and Chattahoochee Rivers. While sending supplies by water would save the government an estimated $2,000 per month, it would also require boats to pass through Spanish Florida and the "Negro Fort" at Prospect Bluff.[8]

Gaines also continued to direct the effort to capture the Red Stick warriors responsible for killing Johnson and McGaskey. The general received intelligence via Camp Montgomery that the Creeks had gone to Prospect Bluff. While he could not verify the reliability of the intelligence, he reported to Jackson that "they are gone to the Appalachacola, and that they carried McGlasky below the line, where they burned him alive by sticking lightwood splinters in his flesh."[9]

The method described for McGaskey's execution was a traditional Creek way of eliminating enemies. Lightwood, typically called "fat light'erd" by residents of the Deep South, comes from the dried stumps and trunks of fallen pines. This wood is so resinous that it will explode into flame almost instantaneously upon contact with fire. Citizens of the region, like the Creeks and Seminoles before them, still use it as fireplace kindling. Burning someone to death by sticking splinters of lightwood into their flesh and setting it ablaze was an excruciating form of torture and execution that had its roots deep in the ancient traditions of the Creek Indians.

Gaines was at Fort Jackson near present-day Wetumpka, Alabama, by April 21, and met there with Col. Benjamin Hawkins. The aging U.S. Agent for Indian Affairs would die just six weeks later. He told Gaines that the Creeks had decided not to oppose the running of the treaty lines, but also had agreed not to provide any assistance or supplies to the survey party. Hawkins also made clear that the maroon settlement at Prospect Bluff was the looming issue in the Creek Nation:

> The Chiefs are making an effort of themselves, to aid the Seminolie Chiefs in destroying the negro establishment

> in that country, capturing and delivering up Negro's belonging to Citizens of the United States, to me, or some of our military establishment. The Little Prince and some warriors are by last report on the march for effecting this object. They have applied for some aid in corn which after conferring with the General is sent them 300 bushels.[10]

Hawkins was personally invested in the destruction of the Fort at Prospect Bluff, as were many of the leading Creek chiefs. Hundreds of slaves from the nation had escaped to the "Negro Fort" during the recently closed War of 1812. Others had joined Red Stick forces during the Creek War and were now moving through the borderlands with the parties of Peter McQueen, Homathlemico and others. Some of Hawkins' own slaves had escaped to Florida and were at Prospect Bluff. While there is no direct evidence that his hopes of recovering them led to his involvement in plans for a Creek raid against the fort, the possibility cannot be ignored.

Officials of the Madison Administration in Washington, D.C. expressed great concern over the maroon settlement in Florida. They instructed Maj. Gen. Jackson to find out what the Spanish at Pensacola planned to do about it. He was at another town named Washington, then the capital of the Mississippi Territory, when he received the orders and immediately wrote to Spanish Governor Mauricio de Zuniga:

> I am charged by my Government to make known to you that a negro fort, erected during our late war with Britain, and at or near the junction of the Chatahoochee and Flint Rivers, has been strengthened since that period, and is now occupied by upwards of two hundred and fifty negroes, many of whom have been enticed from the service of their masters, citizens of the United States; all of whom are well clothed and disciplined. Secret practices to inveigle negroes from the citizens of Georgia, as well as from the Cherokee and Creek nations of Indians, are still continued by this banditti and the hostile Creeks. This is a state of things

> which cannot fail to produce much injury in the neighboring settlements, and excite irritations which eventually may endanger the peace of the nation, and interrupt that good understanding which so happily exists between our Governments.[11]

Zuniga and Jackson knew each other. The former had been in command at Pensacola when U.S. troops seized the city in 1814 and drove out the British troops of Lt. Col. Edward Nicolls. Jackson attacked Pensacola after the British used the city as a base for a military operation against Fort Bowyer at Mobile Point. The amphibious assault had been a violation of Spanish neutrality and Jackson believed it authorized his march on the Spanish capital. He took the city, but was praised by Zuniga and other leaders for the mercy that the American troops showed to the inhabitants. Jackson's kind treatment generated goodwill with Zuniga and the two were now able to communicate about the Negro Fort and the mutual desire of both nations that it be destroyed and its occupants returned to slavery:

> ...The principals of good faith, which always insure good neighborhood between nations, require the immediate and prompt interference of the Spanish authority to destroy or remove from our frontier this banditti, put an end to an evil of so serious a nature, and return to our citizens and friendly Indians inhabiting our territory those negroes now in said fort, and which have been stolen and enticed from them. I cannot permit myself to indulge a belief that the Governor of Pensacola, or the military commander at that place, will hesitate a moment in giving orders for this banditti to be dispersed, and the property of the citizens of the United States forthwith restored to them and our friendly Indians; particularly when I reflect that the conduct of this banditti is such as will not be tolerated by our Government, and, if not put down by Spanish authority, will compel us, in self-defence, to destroy them.[12]

Jackson's view of the fort as a threat to slavery is self-evident in his demand, as is his view of its garrison. He entrusted the letter to Capt. Ferdinand Louis Amelung of the 1st U.S. Infantry, ordering him to deliver it in person and wait for the Governor's response.

It took Amelung more than one month to reach Pensacola from the Mississippi River due to bad weather and problems in obtaining transportation. On the Chattahoochee River, meanwhile, Creek chiefs learned that the United States was considering the construction of another fort, this one far below Fort Gaines on the Spanish border. The Little Prince (Tustunuggee Hopoi), speaker for the Lower Creeks, went to Fort Gaines to personally object to such a move. He spoke to Clinch through interpreter William Hambly, an employee of John Forbes & Company and former lieutenant in Nicolls' battalion of Colonial Marines. He complained that authorities had not discussed plans to build new forts with him and other Creek chiefs:

> ...Jackson and Hawkins spoke to us, and told us we were their children. At the Tuskeegee meeting you told us you would have the land as far down as the Summochichoba; but we chiefs did not agree to it. You did not tell us then you would build forts along the river bank down to the fork; but we heard, since, you issued orders to that effect. We do not think it friendly for one friend to take any thing from another forcibly. The commander and Hawkins did not tell us any thing about building these forts. We hear of your meeting at Tuskeegee. We hope you will detain the forces they are at present, and wait on the Indians, as I am sure they will be able to settle every thing; but all the chiefs are not yet met. You know that we are slow in our movements.[13]

Fort Gaines, 1816

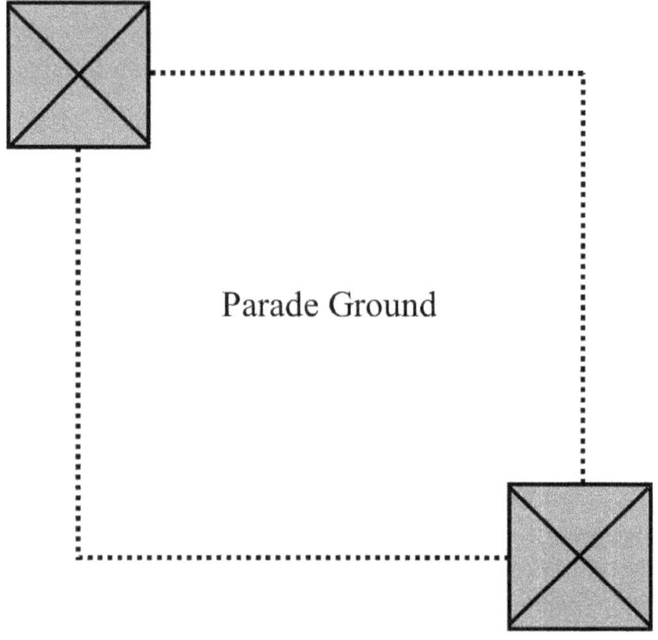

Stockade Wall

Blockhouse

The Prince asked that his talk be sent to Col. Hawkins and Gen. Jackson. He also requested that he be supplied with ink and paper so that he could continue to correspond with American leaders.[14]

The objections of the powerful Creek leader did not deter Gaines and Clinch from planning to send troops from Fort Gaines to the forks of the Chattahoochee and Flint Rivers. Gaines wrote to Clinch on April 28, ordering him to collect as much beef as possible at the fort in order to save his barrels of salted pork for an emergency. He also suggested that Clinch begin the process of fortifying his flatboats with higher sides that could withstand rifle and musket fire from Creek warriors. The possibility of an attack against Clinch was very much on the general's mind.[15]

Fort Gaines would play a critical role in the army's movement down the Chattahoochee River and the coming U.S. campaign against the Negro Fort at Prospect Bluff.

---

[1] Maj. Gen. Edmund P. Gaines to Maj. Gen. Andrew Jackson, April 18, 1816, Andrew Jackson papers, 1775-1874, Library of Congress.
[2] *Ibid.*
[3] *Ibid.*; Lt. Col. Matthew Arbuckle to Maj. Gen. Edmund P. Gaines, November 30, 1817, Andrew Jackson papers, Library of Congress.
[4] 1819 Survey of District 5 of the original Early County, Georgia State Archives.
[5] Bvt. Major Enos Cutler to the Adjutant and Inspector General, April 5, 1816, Adjutant General, Letters Received, NARA.
[6] Maj. Gen. Edmund P. Gaines to Maj. Gen. Andrew Jackson, April 18, 1816, Andrew Jackson Papers, 1775-1874, Library of Congress.
[7] Extract of a letter from an officer at Fort Gaines to a gentleman in Raleigh, April 16, 1816, appeared in the Massachusetts Salem Gazette, p. 2. On May 21, 1816.
[8] Gaines to Jackson, March 18, 1816.
[9] Maj. Gen. Edmund P. Gaines to Maj. Gen. Andrew Jackson, April 18, 1816, Andrew Jackson papers, 1775-1874, Library of Congress.
[10] Benjamin Hawkins to Maj. Gen. Andrew Jackson, April 21, 1816.
[11] Maj. Gen. Andrew Jackson to the Governor of Pensacola, April 23, 1816, American State Papers, Foreign Relations, Volume IV, p. 499.
[12] *Ibid.*

[13] Talk from the Little Prince, Tustunnuggee Hopoi, to the Commander of the United States forces in the Indian nation, April 27, 1816, *American State Papers*, Foreign Relations, Volume IV, p. 558.
[14] *Ibid.*
[15] Maj. Gen. Edmund P. Gaines to Lt. Col. Duncan L. Clinch, April 28, 1816, Andrew Jackson papers, Library of Congress.

CHAPTER THREE

Raiders at Fort Gaines

Fort Gaines was to play one of the most critical roles in its history during April and May of 1816. The position of the fort deep in Indian country on the line dividing the Creek Nation from the new "public lands" seized by the United States via the Treaty of Fort Jackson made it an ideal base of operations. Red Stick war parties continued to linger in the treaty lands. Clinch's command at the fort was expected to be a major force in pacifying these groups. And then, of course, there was the issue of the maroon fort at Prospect Bluff.

Rumors of a Creek expedition against the establishment had been prevalent on the frontier since the final months of the War of 1812. The movement, to be led by William McIntosh, had been delayed for one cause or another but appeared to be on the verge of marching by the spring of 1816. The ailing Col. Benjamin Hawkins, however caused yet another delay when he failed to send a written requisition for 300 bushels of corn that the warriors would need for their expedition into Spanish Florida. Clinch and Gaines worked to correct this bureaucratic logjam even as they prepared for a movement of their own.[1]

Writing from his headquarters at Fort Gaines, Lt. Col. Clinch had proposed that he descend the Chattahoochee River from that point by boat and build a new post directly on the Spanish border. He would destroy any Red Stick towns encountered and then move up the Flint River as far as Burges's Bluff at today's Bainbridge. General Gaines approved the play on April 28, 1816, but urged Clinch to exercise caution:

> Until you are perfectly satisfied as to the strength and healthiness of the position which you may select for a permanent post, you may limit yourself to a temporary work, as I have before suggested, to be thrown up at a convenient point for the present security of your command, until you have it in your power to select a proper site for the intended fort. You will probably find a handsome and suitable bluff on the left or East side of the junction of the rivers. Examine and report to me the situation of the Country at, and for eight or ten miles above the junction, - upon and adjacent to the rivers – noting the different sites which appear to you most eligible – the distance of each from the river, & from the junction of the two.[2]

Implied but not actually stated in the general's letter was a belief that the new post would be a forward base for operations against the fort at Prospect Bluff. The confluence of the Chattahoochee and Flint Rivers forms the Apalachicola River, which then flows south past the site of the maroon settlement. If the Creeks and Seminoles appeared ready to oppose the construction of the new fort with force, Clinch was to halt his movement until an additional battalion of the 4th Infantry could arrive from Charleston. He was then to lead his command down the Chattahoochee from Fort Gaines while the other battalion made its way down the Flint. The two wings of the regiment would meet at the forks.[3]

Gaines cautioned his subordinate to be on guard. "He who acts otherwise, among savages," the general wrote, "not only places himself at the disposal of fortune, but invites insult and disaster."[4]

The Creeks also continued their own effort for a march on the Negro Fort. General Gaines reported to the Secretary of War on April 30, 1816, that the Little Prince had gone down the Chattahoochee River to visit the chiefs living near the Florida line:

> The ostensible object of the visit was to adopt measures to take the negro fort; and as Colonel Hawkins had confidence in the promises of the Indians to effect this object, I sanctioned a requisition for supplying them with three hundred bushels of corn, to serve as rations. That I have little faith in their promises, I will not deny; but it seemed to me proper to encourage them in the prosecution of a measure which I felt persuaded would, if successful, be attended with great benefit to our southern frontier inhabitants, as well as the Indians themselves.[5]

The Prince's mission was less than successful. The towns on the lower river agreed not to oppose his expedition, but they declined to take part in it. The only real exception was Lafarka or John Blunt, a refugee chief from Alabama who had established himself at Iola on the west side of the Apalachicola River. Blunt had been an ally of the British during the War of 1812 but now saw the writing on the wall. He agreed to help any force that might go against the fort at Prospect Bluff.

An officer at Fort Gaines soon reported that the Little Prince's mission had come to a climactic end. The news that the chief brought back from Florida was so alarming that the garrison prepared to defend against an immediate attack:

> ...The Little Prince, and all the chiefs of the friendly party, have been below endeavoring to make friends of the hostile party, but without effect; the night before last a chief of the Seminoles made his appearance at the council house with 200 warriors, and dissolved their meeting, firing and threatening to put the friendly chiefs to death if they did not

> leave there immediately; some of the friendly chiefs passed here to-day on their way home.[6]

The same officer reported that a serious incident had taken place just two miles from Fort Gaines on May 1st. Several supply wagons were making their way from the post back to Fort Hawkins when they were stopped by a small party of warriors. One of the wagon drivers managed to escape and ran the two miles back to the fort to sound the alarm. The unnamed officer led 30 volunteers out to save the wagons. They arrived so quickly that the lives of the other wagon drivers were saved. The wagons were soon on the move again for Fort Hawkins, this time under the escort of the officer and his men. The war party, however, continued to hover in the vicinity:

> ...[D]uring my absence, the same party was guilty of one of the most daring outrages I ever heard of; while two men, belonging to my company, were attending 30 cattle belonging to us, within half a mile of camp, about 12 o'clock, at noon, they were driven off along with two public horses; we sent a small party in pursuit, but without coming up with them; they took the road on to St. Marks, crossing Flint river about 20 miles from its mouth. I have no doubt but that it is a small party of Seminoles or [Mc]Queens party. I regret the loss of the two poor fellows, as I have no doubt they are scalped before this, it being unusual for the Indians to keep prisoners.[7]

The McQueen mentioned in the letter was Peter McQueen, a major leader of Red Stick forces during the Creek War of 1813-1814. He had escaped into Florida following the destruction of a key Red Stick army at the Battle of Horseshoe Bend. There he allied with the British forces of Lt. Col. Edward Nicolls and served with them until the end of the War of 1812. He was still in Florida at the head of several hundred Red Stick warriors in 1816. Jackson, Gaines and other U.S. leaders considered him to be an absolute threat.[8]

Rumors soon reached Fort Gaines that 250 Red Stick and Seminole warriors had gathered about 40 miles below the post. An attack was expected and the anonymous officer warned friends in the settled areas that "you may expect to hear of some scalping in this quarter very soon." There were fewer than 300 effective men at the fort, although he noted that Fort Gaines was protected by three good cannon, "2 six pounders and a 4."[9]

The capture of the soldiers at Fort Gaines was a major concern for American officers, as was the loss of the herd they had been driving. Lt. Col. Clinch sent a spy in pursuit of the raiding party. That individual returned to the fort on May 5 with word that the warriors had crossed the Flint River "at Burges's old place," a reference to the former trading post of James Burges at what is now Bainbridge, Georgia. The two soldiers were still alive but the spy warned that they would be killed if they became too tired to keep up with the movements of their captors. He believed that they were being taken to Prospect Bluff.[10]

The unidentified scout reported that war was imminent:

> …He further states that he understood from some of his friends in that quarter, that the Semilones, all the Towns on the Flint near the Confluence of the two rivers, and most of those on the Chattohoochee were preparing for war – that they had been dancing and drinking their war Physic for several days that they had determined to divide themselves into two parties, one party to go against Hartford (Georgia) and the other to come up and attack the Troops under my Command. This rumour has been confirmed by an Indian just from Flint, who arrived at the Town of the Oketeyocannes last evening, the Chief of which town sent W. Hardridge who lives near him to me this morning, to inform me that such were the reports but that he did not know what to think of them.[11]

The "W. Hardridge" mentioned in the above report was William Hardridge, a white trader and sometimes assistant Indian agent who lived near Fort Gaines. He told Lt. Col. Clinch that a major division was taking place in the lower towns. Those who wished to remain at peace with the United States were preparing to relocate upriver to within the new limits of the Creek Nation. The rest - numbering 1,500 to 2,000 warriors - were determined on war. William Hambly confirmed the strength of the pro-war party when he told Clinch that the British had organized a force of 3,000 Creeks, Seminoles and Choctaws during their sojourn on the Apalachicola. "If they are determined on a fight," wrote the lieutenant colonel, "I feel every disposition to gratify them."[12]

Little Prince's return to Fort Gaines had been hastened by a pursuing party of warriors from Fowltown. His effort to obtain support for an attack on the Negro Fort had failed, he told Clinch, because "they were crazy, and would not listen to him." The Prince, Hambly and their escort barely escaped with their lives after the Red Sticks threatened to burn them to death.[13]

> ...The Tuttolosees and Miccosookus, are the principal instigators, but he thinks most of the Towns on the Flint, below Barnetts, and several towns on the East Bank of the Chattohoochie will join them. Several of the chiefs below and near me have come in and begged protection, they state that they have their crops in the ground, and unless I will let them stay at home and till them, their women and children must starve. I have told them to stay at home and make their corn, that when I approached their towns, the Chiefs must meet me with their warriors without arms, that I would take a list of them, and if any of them joined the hostile party, they were never to suffer them to return again, on pain on having their towns destroyed.[14]

The chiefs agreed to the conditions demanded by Clinch. The Little Prince reported that he had ordered the leaders of all towns wishing to remain at peace with the whites to report themselves to Fort Gaines at once.

Lt. Col. Clinch was as eager to go to war as his Red Stick and Seminole counterparts. He immediately proposed that two companies from the second battalion of the 4th Infantry then on the march from Charleston be sent to reinforce him. He wanted put the hostile towns to the torch:

> ...I then propose leaving all my heavy baggage, and a sufficient number of men to man the boats at this post, and move the balance of my command down the river by rapid marches, and destroy every hostile town between this and the Confluence of the two rivers, after which my boats can drop down with ease and safety in two days. I will then select a strong position on the Flint, fortify my Camp, move up that river, and destroy all the Towns to Burgess old place, and order the Command left at the Agency to descend the Flint with our supplies, and if my force will admit of it; I will pursue the enemy further, and strike a blow in another quarter.[15]

Clinch's vague reference to striking a blow in "another quarter" was un undoubtedly a reference to the fort at Prospect Bluff. The "Negro Fort," as the Americans called it, was also on the minds of Edmund Gaines and Andrew Jackson. Gaines wrote to Jackson on May 14, reporting that he had "reconnoitering parties" operating from each post along the frontier looking for the murderers of Johnson and McGaskey. One of these posts was Fort Gaines. Meanwhile, he reported, the first part of the campaign to take the Negro Fort was underway:

> The Little Prince with other chiefs and Warriors have engaged to take the Negro Fort on the Apa'la'cha'co'la and deliver the negroes at 50$ each. Col. Hawkins is of the opinion they will succeed, and although I have little faith in Indian promises, it seems to me proper to encourage the undertaking and wait a reasonable time for the result. I have sanctioned Col. Hawkins requisition for 300 bushels of

> corn for the subsistence of the Indians. They are not however to be considered as in our service or entitled to Pay. Should they fail, I shall then avail myself of the discretionary power which you have been pleased to confide to me and shall adopt such measures as may appear best Calculated to Counteract Indian hostility and at the same time to break up the Negro establishment, which I have reason to believe is acquiring strength and additional numbers.[16]

American troops were now converging on the frontier. Captain Alex Cummings was on the march to Fort Hawkins from Charleston, South Carolina, with the final battalion of the 4th Infantry. Two companies of light artillery were preparing to march and on the border north of Pensacola Major David E. Twiggs was finally in route to build the long-awaited fort near the Conecuh.[17]

General Gaines, meanwhile, initiated the main U.S. operation against the fort at Prospect Bluff. He explained the situation in a letter to Commodore Daniel Patterson of the U.S. Navy on May 22, 1816. Patterson was the senior naval officer at New Orleans and his approval was required for U.S. warships to escort the supply vessels that he was sending to the Apalachicola with provisions and other necessities for Fort Gaines as well as the proposed post at the forks. The general went onto detail the capture of the two soldiers at Fort Gaines and the murders of Johnson and McGaskey before mentioning his plans to build a new fort near the head of the Apalachicola:

> …I have determined upon an experiment by water, and for this purpose have to request your co-operation; should you feel authorized to detach a small gun-vessel or two as a convoy to the boats charged with our supplies up the Appalachicola, I am persuaded that, in doing so, you will contribute much to the benefit of the service, and the accommodation of my immediate command in this quarter.

> The transports will be under the direction of the officer of the gun-vessel, and the whole should be provided against an attack by small arms from shore. To guard against accidents, I will direct Lieutenant Colonel Clinch to have in readiness a boat sufficient to carry fifty men, to meet the vessels on the river and assist them up.[18]

The general provided Patterson with as much information as he could on the construction and armament of the Prospect Bluff fort, telling the commodore that if the passage of the ships was greeted with opposition from the inhabitants of the fort, "it shall be destroyed."[19]

One day later Gaines ordered Clinch to begin his descent of the Chattahoochee River from Fort Gaines. "If your supplies of provisions and ammunition have reached you," the general wrote from Camp Montgomery near the former site of Fort Mims, "let your detachment move as directed in my letter of the 28th of last month." The soldiers were to carry with them twenty-five days' rations with more provisions to follow via boat from Fort Gaines. The force was to move with caution:

> ...The force of the whole nation cannot arrest your movement down the river on board the boats, if secured up the sides with two-inch plank, and covered over with clapboards; nor could all the nation prevent your landing and constructing a stockade work, sufficient to secure you, unless they should previously know the spot at which you intended to land, and had actually assembled at that place previous to or within four hours of your landing; but your force is not sufficient to warrant your march to the different villages, as suggested, by land. The whole of your force (except about forty men, or one company, for the defence of Fort Gaines) should be kept near your boats and supplies until the new post shall be established. You may then strike at any hostile party near you, with all your disposable force;

> but even then you should not go more than one or two days' march from your fort.[20]

Gaines did not trust William Hambly and cautioned Clinch to be careful of intelligence received from the former British lieutenant. He worried that the interpreter might still be a spy or agent of Lt. Col. Nicolls.[21]

The general updated Clinch on the movement of the ships being sent with supplies and also indicated that heavy guns were being sent to help in the reduction of the fort at Prospect Bluff:

> ...Should the boats meet with opposition at what is called the Negro fort, arrangements will immediately be made for its destruction; and for that purpose you will be supplied with two eighteen-pounders and one howitzer, with fixed ammunition and implements complete, to be sent in a vessel to accompany the provisions. I have, likewise, ordered fifty thousand musket cartridges, some rifles, swords, &c. Should you be compelled to go against the negro fort, you will land at a convenient point above it, and force a communication with the commanding officer of the vessels below, and arrange with him your plan of attack. Upon this subject you shall hear from me again, as soon as I am notified of the time at which the vessels will sail from New Orleans.[22]

The first step, of course, would be the establishment of the new fort at the head of the Apalachicola. "The post near the junction of the rivers, to which I called your attention last month," Gaines wrote to Clinch, "must be established speedily." This was an essential task, he continued, "even if we have to fight our way through the ranks of the whole nation."[23]

Communications of the time were slow and it would take time for these orders to travel across the modern state of Alabama to Fort Gaines. As the courier made his way forward, Captain Amelung finally reached Pensacola with General Jackson's letter to Governor Mauricio de Zuniga. The Spanish official replied on May 26 providing Jackson with basic information on the location and history of the fort at Prospect Bluff. Zuniga also explained that Spanish citizens were even more aggrieved by its existence than those of the United States. Nicolls and Woodbine, he reported, had carried away many slaves belonging to Spanish residents of Florida. The governor was willing to move against the fort if properly authorized, reinforced and supplied from Cuba. He had applied to the Captain General for these things and assured Jackson that his thinking "exactly corresponds with yours as to the dislodging of the negroes from the fort, the occupying it with Spanish troops, or destroying it, and delivering the negroes who may be collected to their lawful owners."[24]

The proposed Spanish expedition would assemble as promised, but events now outpaced both Jackson and Zuniga. Clinch received his orders from Gaines and began to make final preparations for his departure from Fort Gaines for the Apalachicola. A bit of good news arrived as these preparations for war went forward. The two soldiers taken near the fort were unexpectedly released by their Red Stick captors. Part of the herd was also sent back as a peace gesture by some of the chiefs. A group of Upper Crek scouts, meanwhile, located two of the alleged killers of Johnson and McGaskey and the accused murderers were jailed at Fort Jackson by June 3, 1816.[25]

Lt. Col. Clinch left Fort Gaines on June 7, 1816, to begin his descent of the Chattahoochee River. He reached the forks two days later and reported on the 12th that he had begun building a new fort on the first suitable bluff up the Flint River. The new post was first named Camp Crawford, but is better remembered by its later name – Fort Scott.

[1] Maj. Gen. Edmund P. Gaines to Lt. Col. Duncan L. Clinch, April 28, 1816, Andrew Jackson papers, Library of Congress.
[2] *Ibid.*
[3] *Ibid.*

[4] *Ibid.*
[5] Maj. Gen. Edmund P. Gaines to Hon. William Crawford, April 30, 1816, *American State Papers*, Foreign Relations, Volume IV, pp. 557-558.
[6] Officer at Fort Gaines to Editors of the Baltimore Patriot, May 5, 1816 (Appeared in the Virginia American Beacon, p. 3., on June 10, 1816).
[7] *Ibid.*
[8] For an account of McQueen's escape into Florida and his subsequent alliance with the British, please see *Nicolls' Outpost*, Old Kitchen Books, 2015, by this author.
[9] Officer at Fort Gaines to Editors of the Baltimore Patriot, May 5, 1816.
[10] Lt. Col. Duncan L. Clinch to Maj. Gen. Edmund P. Gaines, May 7, 1816, Andrew Jackson papers, Library of Congress.
[11] *Ibid.*
[12] *Ibid.*
[13] Lt. Col. Duncan L. Clinch to Maj. Gen. Edmund P. Gaines, May 9, 1816, Andrew Jackson papers, Library of Congress.
[14] *Ibid.*
[15] Lt. Col. Duncan L. Clinch to Maj. Gen. Edmund P. Gaines, May 9, 1816, Andrew Jackson papers, Library of Congress.
[16] Maj.Gen. Edmund P. Gaines to Maj. Gen. Andrew Jackson, May 14, 1816, Andrew Jackson papers, Library of Congress.
[17] *Ibid.*, *North Carolina Star*, May 31, 1816, p. 2.
[18] Maj. Gen. Edmund P. Gaines to Commodore Daniel T. Patterson, May 22, 1816, American State Papers, Foreign Affairs, Volume IV, p. 559.
[19] *Ibid.*
[20] Maj. Gen. Edmund P. Gaines to Lt. Col. Duncan L. Clinch, May 23, 1816, American State Papers, Foreign Affairs, Volume IV, p. 558.
[21] *Ibid.*
[22] *Ibid.*
[23] *Ibid.*
[24] Gov. Mauricio de Zuniga to Maj. Gen. Andrew Jackson, May 26, 1816, American State Papers, Foreign Affairs, Volume IV, pp. 499-500.
[25] Maj. Gen. Edmund P. Gaines to Maj. Gen. Andrew Jackson, June 3, 1816, Andrew Jackson Papers, Library of Congress.

CHAPTER FOUR

Fort Scott and the Negro Fort

The summer of 1816 was one of the most dramatic in American history. A plume of ash from a volcanic explosion in the Pacific Ocean encircled the earth, giving the sky an eerie red hue and temporarily but drastically changing the climate of the Northern Hemisphere. Temperatures plunged and the planting season came very late that year. Snow was reported in New England as late as June while river ice was reported in Pennsylvania as late as July. Frost occurred in Virginia in July and cold easterly winds left people huddling by their fires throughout the South.

It was against the backdrop of this "year without a summer" that the soldiers from Fort Gaines arrived at the forks of the Chattahoochee and Flint Rivers and built the temporary work that they called Camp Crawford. The Creek chief John Blunt met with Lt. Col. Clinch there and then set out for Apalachicola Bay on June 17, 1816. He bore instructions for the commander of the expected U.S. Navy flotilla to remain at anchor in the bay until Clinch could bring troops down to assist the vessels in passing the Negro Fort at Prospect Bluff. Gunboats #149 and #154, meanwhile, set sail from New Orleans in late June. They met with the supply vessels *Semelante* and *General Pike* at Pass Christian and proceeded in convoy for the Apalachicola.[1]

At roughly the same time, an editorial from Milledgeville, Georgia, spread northward through the nation's newspapers. It included a clarion call for the destruction of the fort at Prospect Bluff:

> It has long been known, that the British station at Appalachicola bay, within the Spanish territory, where Nicolls concentrated his force and erected a fort, has, since he evacuated it, been held by runaway negroes and hostile Indians, who have done and continue to do mischief to the whites, as occasion and opportunity offer. It was not to have been expected, that an establishment so pernicious to the southern states, holding out to a part of their population temptations to insubordination, would have been suffered to exist after the close of the war. In the course of the last winter several slaves from this neighborhood fled to that fort; others have lately gone from Tennessee and the Mississippi territory. How long shall this evil, requiring immediate remedy, be permitted to exist? If the Spaniards connive at this nuisance, shall we out of respect to them (suffering from its present ills and anticipating greater) continue to tolerate it? True, it is within their territorial limits, and as good neighbors, they should disperse this horde of ruffians, and deliver up the slaves to their owners. But if they decline to do so or are dilatory about it, we can discover no reason why the regular troops, of them there are more than enough in the nation, should not be ordered on that service with the least possible delay.[2]

How much the writer knew about the plans then unfolding for the destruction of the fort is not known. His proposed plan, however, was so similiar to the plan being implemented by General Gaines and Lt. Col. Clinch that he was probably familiar with their efforts. "A few hundred men sent down the river and some gun boats up the bay," he wrote, "would readily effect the object."[3]

With the U.S. Navy closing in on Apalachicola, operations also got underway on the Chattahoochee. The long awaited movement of Creek forces against the Negro Fort began with the warriors advancing in two bodies under the commands of William McIntosh and Captain Isaacs. The former individual had fought alongside U.S. forces during the Creek War of 1813-1814 and bore the military rank of major. The latter had been a Red Stick prophet who switched sides:

> We learn by gentlemen from the westward, that a party of the Creek warriors, from 500 to 1000 strong, under their gallant chief M'Intosh, contemplated marching early this month against the hostile Indians in Florida, (the Seminoles) and had given assurance that they would capture and destroy the obnoxious Fort on Appalachicola Bay – most of the hostile Indians were said to be on a visit at Pensacola, where 600 Spanish troops had lately arrived.[4]

The timing of the movement of the Creeks under Maj. William McIntosh either preplanned or a remarkable coincidence. Military reports indicate that the warriors moved out on their own without prior coordination with Lt. Col. Clinch. This is certainly possible, but McIntosh and other chiefs undoubtedly knew that U.S. troops had dropped down the Chattahoochee to the confluence. The launch of the Creek expedition, however, meant that three strong forces were closing in on the fort at Prospect Bluff, two by land and one by sea. The exact date on which the warriors left the vicinity of Fort Mitchell to begin their downriver march is not known.

The gunboats and their charges reached Apalachicola Bay on July 10, 1816. Five days later the lookouts spotted a small boat off the site of today's city of Apalachicola. A brief skirmish followed with no obvious injury to either side, making clear that the maroons intended to fight.

Chief Blunt reached Camp Crawford on the same day with news of the arrival of the ships. Clinch immediately sent him back down to let Sailing

Master Jairus Loomis know that the soldiers were coming. His men spent July 16, 1816, loading supplies aboard their flatboats and equipping themselves with rations, arms and ammunition for the expedition. McIntosh and Isaacs passed Fort Gaines at about the same time. Although details of their movement are sparse, they chiefs and their warriors likely obtained additional provisions at the post before continuing down the river to the forks. Clinch left Camp Crawford by boat on the following morning with 116 chosen men:

> ...The Detachment was divided in two companies commanded by B. Major Muhlenberg and Capt. Taylor. On the same evening I was joined by Major McIntosh with one hundred and fifty Indians, and on the 18th day by an old chief called Capt. Isaacs and the celebrated Chief Kotcha-hajo or Mad Tiger at the head of a large body of Indians many of whom were without arms. My junction with these Chiefs was accidental their expedition having been long since projected. Their object was to capture the negroes within the Fort, and return them to their proper owners.[5]

As the soldiers and warriors were moving for the forks, a party of maroons and Choctaw warriors attacked a boat party sent into the mouth of the Apalachicola River in search of fresh water. A midshipman and two sailors were killed, a fourth man was taken prisoner and a fifth managed to escape by swimming away. The captured seaman, Edward Daniels, was carried back to Prospect Bluff where he was "tarred and burnt alive."[6]

Lt. Col. Clinch, meanwhile, was continuing his movement down the Apalachicola River. He met with McIntosh, Mad Tiger and Captain Isaacs on the 18th and reached an agreement for the Creek and U.S. forces to cooperate in their attack on the fort. Lt. Kendal Lewis of McIntosh's command served as interpreter and the resulting document was short and to the point:

> Art. 1 We agree to unite in reducing the Negro Fort.

Art. 2 In case the Fort should be taken the Indians are to have all the Powder (cannon excepted) small arms, clothing &c. & Fifty Dollars for every ground Negro taken by them, not the property of the Creek Nation.

Art. 3 Lt. Col. D.L. Clinch is to take possession in the name of the U. States of all the Cannon, Ordnance Stores &c. & all the property the Indians cannot carry from the Fort.[7]

Clinch sent the Creeks down the east side of the river with scout parties moving ahead of the main columns. A few soldiers from the 4th Infantry were sent to join them. The slow-moving flatboats meanwhile continued down the river. It was not long before the Creeks intercepted a messenger on his way from the bluff to Fowltown and Miccosukee to seek reinforcements:

> …On the 19th they brought in a prisoner taken the evening before. He had a scalp which he said he was carrying to the Seminoles. – He further stated that the Black Commandant and the Choctaw Chief had returned to the Fort from the Bay the day before, with a party of men, with information that they had killed several Americans and taken a Boat from them. I was met the same day by Lafarka who informed me that he had not been able to deliver my second letter to the officer commanding the Gun Vessels.[8]

The fate of the courier is unknown, but the Creek forces continued to capture other escaped slaves as they advanced. As many as 100, most of them claimed by Native American owners, were taken over the next two days.

> …At two o'clock on the morning of the 20th we landed within cannon shot of the Fort, but protected by a skirt of

> woods. I again sent Lafarka with a letter notifying the officer commanding the convoy of my arrival. My plan of attack was communicated to the Chiefs, and a party of Indians under Major McIntosh were directed to surround the Fort. Finding it impossible to carry my plans into execution without the assistance of Artillery, I ordered Major McIntosh to keep one third of his men constantly hovering around the fort and to keep up an irregular fire – this had the desired effect as it induced the enemy to amuse us with an incessant roar of Artillery without any other effect than that of striking terror into the souls of most of our red friends.[9]

One look at the fort was all it took for Lt. Col. Clinch to realize that his original plan of taking it with 80 men was impossible. Even with more than 300 soldiers and Creek warriors now at his disposal, the walls of the fort were too strong to storm without first breaching them with heavy artillery.

Prospect Bluff was not a soaring height as described by some authors, but it was extremely well fortified. Natural creeks, branches and swamps ringed its landward sides and the defenses themselves were designed to present a layered system of moats, trenches, breastworks, stockades and heavy walls to any attacking force. A wide field of fire had been cleared around the works and strong bastions allowed for musket and cannon fire to sweep the approaches to all three of its land faces. Inside the bastioned outer line were additional stockade lines, a moat and finally an octagonal citadel built of earth and logs. An earthwork water battery faced the river. Three magazines were positioned at strategic points in the complex, the largest being in the central octagon which also contained storehouses for weapons, offices and other rooms.

Although accounts of the battle often list a garrison of 300-320 men for the fort, that figure includes women and children. The total number of men in the fort was only 80-100, including the 20 or so Choctaw warriors. Women and some of the older children, however, joined in manning the artillery as it became clear they were fighting for their freedom and their lives.

Loomis began to warp his vessels up the river a few days later and reached what he called "Duelling Bluff" about four miles below Prospect Bluff on the July 25,1816. This was undoubtedly the low elevation known today as Bloody Bluff. The naval officer found his army counterpart waiting there and welcomed him aboard Gunboat #149:

> ...[H]e informed me that in attempting to pass within gun shot of the fortifications, he had been fired upon by the negroes, and that he had also been fired upon for the last four or five days, whenever any of his troops appeared in view; we immediately reconnoitered the fort, and determined on a site to erect a small battery of two eighteen pounders, to assist the gun vessels to force the navigation of the river, as it was evident from their hostility, we should be obliged to do.[10]

The final attack on the fort took place on the morning of July 27, 1816. Clinch and his men had spent the previous day preparing a site for an intended battery on the west bank of the river almost 2 miles below the fort.. Loomis write that he planned to convey the *Semelante* up under cover of darkness to land the guns but instead found himself embroiled in debate with the lieutenant colonel over whether it was worth the effort:

> ...[H]e however stated to me, that he was not acquainted with artillery, but that he thought the distance was too great to do execution; on this subject we unfortunately differed totally in opinion, as we were within point blank range, he however ordered his men to desist from further operations; I then told him that the gun vessels would attempt the passage of the fort, in the morning *without his aid*.[11]

Clinch and Loomis later engaged in a heated debate over the facts as given by the naval officer, but both agreed on what happened when the gunboats came within view of the fort on the morning of the 27th:

> ...About six in the morning they came up in handsome stile and made fast along side of the intended battery. In a few minutes they received a shot from a thirty two pounder which was returned in a gallant manner. The contest was but momentary, the fifth discharge a hot shot from Gun Vessel 154 commanded by sailing Master Bassett entered the magazine and blew up the Fort.[12]

The explosion of the fort at Prospect Bluff had a lasting impact on most if not all of those who witnessed it. Clinch himself was clearly shocked by the aftermath:

> ...The explosion was awful and the scene horrible beyond description. Our first care on arriving at the scene of destruction was to rescue and relieve the unfortunate beings that survived the explosion. The war yells of the Indians, the cries and lamentations of the wounded compelled the soldier to pause in the midst of victory and to drop a tear for the sufferings of his fellow beings, and to acknowledge that the Great Ruler of the Universe must have used us as his instrument in chastising the blood-thirsty and murderous wretches that defended the Fort.[13]

Other officers gave similar accounts. Dr. Marcus Buck, a surgeon from the 4th Infantry, tried to help the handful of survivors:

> ...You cannot conceive, nor I describe the horrors of the scene. In an instant, hundreds of lifeless bodies were stretched upon the plain, buried in sand and rubbish, or suspended from the tops of the surrounding pines. Here lay

> an innocent babe, there a helpless mother; on the one side a sturdy warrior, on the other a bleeding squaw. Piles of bodies, large heaps of sand, broken guns, accoutrements, &c. covered the scite of the fort. The brave soldier was disarmed of his resentment, and checked his victorious career, to drop a tear on the distressing scene.[14]

It was estimated by the officers present that 270 men, women and children died in the explosion. Another 50 or so were injured and many of these died of their wounds. Only seven of the survivors proved to have come from the United States. The others were from Pensacola and St. Augustine or had previously lived in the Seminole and Creek towns. At least one was from Jamaica.[15]

Clinch had promised McIntosh, Isaacs and Mad Tiger that they could have all the captured small arms and powder that they could carry away. This proved to be a massive haul. An inventory prepared by army and navy officers included a wide variety of tools, shoes, uniforms, etc., as well as 550 muskets and twelve pieces of artillery. Another 2,500 muskets could not be salvaged. Cannon shot was so scattered across the scene that the officers did not even attempt to collect and inventory it. They did save 163 barrels of powder, all of which was claimed by the Creeks.[16]

The cargo of the supply vessel *General Pike* was transferred to Clinch's flatboats for the trip up to Camp Crawford and Fort Gaines. Some of the cargo from the *Semelante* was also placed aboard the flatboats in order to lighten the schooner enough for her to make the trip upriver at least as far as the forks. The soldiers also took a number of shovels, pick axes and other tools from the fort, along with a 5.5 inch brass howitzer, two casks of gunflints, 50 muskets and other items. The rest of the captured artillery and supplies was loaded aboard the naval vessels and the *General Pike* for transport to New Orleans.[17]

Clinch's troops began their return to Camp Crawford on July 30, 1816. Two days later they were warned of a potential attack by outraged Red Stick and Seminole warriors:

> …I received information that a large body of Seminole Indians were within a day's march of us, and in a few hours the report was confirmed by a letter from Major Cutler left in command at Camp Crawford informing me that a large body of Seminoles were descending the Appalachicola. I immediately ordered Major Muhlenburgh to keep the boats together, and to be in readiness to receive them, and directed one hundred Indians to keep with the Boats, and to act in concert if necessary. I advanced with two hundred Cowetas under the gallant Major McIntosh to meet them, but the cowardly wretches dispersed without our being able to get a view of them.[18]

Dr. Buck reported that the Native Americans had planned to attack the rear of Clinch's force and break the siege of the fort at Prospect Bluff. The explosion took place so quickly, however, that they withdrew from the river and "sent word that they wished to make peace."[19]

The troops reached Camp Crawford on August 2, 1816. Some of the supplies and captured material was unloaded there, along with the howitzer and two heavy guns sent from New Orleans. Other material continued up to Fort Gaines by flatboat for the use of the garrison there. Eight captured African American men were placed in confinement:

Names		Owners	
Lamb		Col. B. Hawkins	
Elijah		Mr. Lewis	Georgia
Abraham		W.B. Howell	do.
Jo		Capt. Bowen	do.
Bature	Owned by a Frenchman living at the bay of St. Louis, M.T.		
Jacob		William Margart	
William		Dulendo a "Jew King" Jamaica	
Charles	Said he belongs to John Tharp, but it is supposed he is owned by some gentlemen in Virginia, as he arrived at		

Pensacola in the English Vessel Sea Horse.[20]

It is telling that Clinch's list included no women or children. Hundreds of these had died in the blast. The lieutenant colonel also tried to explain the failure of the expedition to find many escaped slaves from the United States by claiming that most had escaped to the Suwannee River ahead of the attack.

One name of great interest appeared on the list of prisoners. The noted maroon chief Abraham was a member of the British Colonial Marines at Prospect Bluff and remained behind when Nicolls evacuated most of the garrison in 1815. He survived the explosion and was taken prisoner but remained in captivity for only a short time. Abraham was on the Suwannee by 1818 and later played a critical role during the Second Seminole War. He was sent west on the Trail of Tears in 1839 and lived the rest of his life on the Little River in what is now Oklahoma. He was still alive there as late as 1870.[21]

The bloody scene at Prospect Bluff had a telling effect on the officers and men of Clinch's command. Two of his surgeons, Drs. Buck and Hall, resigned almost immediately upon their return to Camp Crawford. Lt. Pendleton resigned while on furlough in Washington, D.C., and Capt. William Taylor likewise announced his intention to resign.[22]

The name of the new outpost was soon changed to Fort Scott, probably in honor of Maj. Gen. Winfield T. Scott. Exactly when the renaming took place is not known, but officers do not seem to have used the name Camp Crawford after October 26, 1816. The timing of the name change coincided closely with the near completion of the new cantonment at the site. Higher authorities, however, believed that the destruction of the fort at Prospect Bluff would intimidate the Red Sticks and Seminoles enough to prevent them from further resisting the survey and settlement of the Fort Jackson treaty lands. Col. William King of the 4th Infantry was ordered to direct the evacuation of Fort Scott and the movement of Lt. Col. Clinch's troops to Camp Montgomery on the Alabama by way of Forts Gaines and Mitchell. The orders reached the Flint River post on November 22, 1816:

> This movement at this season of the year is as strange as to me unaccountable. The troops had just got into their winter quarters when I left them for F.H. [Fort Hawkins] where I expected to have had the pleasure of seeing you, but on my arrival found a letter from Colo. King informing me that the order for the movement of the Regt. would be sent to me from F. Montgomery, on his arrival at that place, which order did not come until the 22d. Ult.[23]

Clinch was greatly alarmed by the timing and nature of the evacuation orders. It was problematic at best to move a large body of troops from comfortable new quarters across a long stretch of unsettled frontier in t coldest weather of the year. Furthermore, Col. King had instructed him to completely abandon Fort Gaines but to leave a subaltern and 24 enlisted men at Fort Scott. Clinch knew that anger was growing among the Seminoles and Red Sticks over the destruction and capture of their supplies at Prospect Bluff and he believed that leaving only 25 men to hold a fort designed for four companies, as the new cantonment at Fort Scott was, would invite their massacre. Abandoning Fort Gaines would leave them completely isolated on a dangerous frontier, far from any source of support or reinforcement. “It would have been better to have them shot at once,” he wrote in a December letter to General Gaines.[24]

The lieutenant colonel set out in person to find and speak with Gen. Gaines, but failed to located him. He then deviated from his orders and completely evacuated Fort Scott but left one company of infantry at Fort Gaines. The latter post was not only small enough to be held by a single company, but it was within range of fast reinforcement from either Fort Mitchell or the allied Creek towns. The mestizo trader George Perryman was left as caretaker at Fort Scott, where some supplies were being left behind, and the last of the troops marched for Fort Gaines in mid to late December of 1816.

[1] Sailing Master Jairus Loomis to Commodore Daniel T. Patterson, August 13, 1816.

[2] *Georgia Journal*, quoted in the South Carolina *City Gazette*, July 4, 1816, p. 2.

[3] *Ibid.*

[4] *Georgia Journal*, July 10, 1816, p. 3.

[5] Lt. Col. Duncan L. Clinch to Col. Robet Butler, Adjutant General, August 2, 1816, Andrew Jackson Papers, Library of Congress.

[6] Sailing Master Jairus Loomis to Commodore Daniel T. Patterson, August 15, 1816.

[7] Articles of Agreement entered into on the 18th July 1816 by Lt. Col. D.L. Clinch on the part of the U.States & the Chiefs Capt. Isaacs, Kotcha harja, & Majr. McIntosh on the part of the Creek Nation, enclosed in Lt. Col. Duncan L. Clinch to Col. Robert Butler, Adjutant General, August 2, 1816.

[8] Lt. Col. Duncan L. Clinch to Col. Robert Butler, Adjutant General, August 2, 1816.

[9] *Ibid.*

[10] *Ibid.*

[11] Sailing Master Jairus Loomis to Commodore Daniel T. Patterson, August 15, 1816.

[12] Lt. Col. Duncan L. Clinch to Col. Robert Butler, Adjutant General, August 2, 1816.

[13] *Ibid.*

[14] Dr. Marcus C. Buck to his father, August 4, 1816, included in "General Clinch and the Indians," *Army and Navy Chronicle*, Volume 2 (New Series), 1836, pp. 114-116.

[15] For a detailed history of the attack and destruction of the fort on the Apalachicola, please see *The Fort at Prospect Bluff* by this author, scheduled for release in the summer of 2016 by Old Kitchen Books.

[16] Inventory of Military Stores captured at the Negro Fort East Florida, July 28, 1816, enclosed in Lt. Col. Duncan L. Clinch to Col. Robert Butler, August 2, 1816, Andrew Jackson Papers, Library of Congress; Lt. Col. Duncan L. Clinch to Col. Robert Butler, Adjutant, August 2, 1816, Andrew Jackson Papers, Library of Congress; Articles of Agreement, July 18, 1816, enclosed in Lt. Col. Duncan L. Clinch to Col. Robert Butler, August 2, 1816, Andrew Jackson Papers, Library of Congress.

[17] Inventory of Military Stores captured at the Negro Fort East Florida, July 28, 1816, enclosed in Lt. Col. Duncan L. Clinch to Col. Robert Butler, August 2, 1816, Andrew Jackson Papers, Library of Congress.

[18] Lt Col. Duncan L. Clinch to Col. Robert Butler, Adjutant, August 2, 1816.

[19] Dr. Marcus C. Buck to his father, August 4, 1816, in "Colonel Clinch and the Indians," *Army and Navy Chronicle,* Volume 2 (New Edition), 1836.

[20] "List of Negroes in Confinement at this Post," August 4, 1816, enclosed in Lt. Col. Duncan L. Clinch to Col. Robert Butler, August 2, 1816, Andrew Jackson Papers, Library of Congress.
[21] Kenneth W. Porter, "The Negro Abraham."
[22] Lt. Col. Duncan L. Clinch to Brig. Gen. Daniel Parker, September 6, 1816, Adjutant General, Letters Received, NARA; Lt. Col. Duncan L. Clinch to Brig. Gen. Daniel Parker, October 5, 1816, Adjutant General, Letters Received, NARA.
[23] Lt. Col. Duncan L. Clinch to Maj. Gen. Edmund P. Gaines, December 26, 1817, Adjutant General, Letters Received, NARA.
[24] *Ibid.*

CHAPTER FIVE

The Winter of 1816-1817

Lt. Col. Duncan Clinch's decision to disobey orders and abandon Fort Scott instead of Fort Gaines likely saved many lives. In addition to the 24 soldiers that would have been left isolated and vulnerable at the former post, new settlers were already flooding in to settle around Fort Gaines. The evacuation of the garrison from the stockade there would have left them completely exposed to attack by the Red Sticks and Seminoles.

Authorities in the nation's capital recognized the folly of their original plan as well. Even before the last of the soldiers left Fort Scott on their march up to Fort Gaines, acting Secretary of War George Graham wrote to Maj. Gen. Jackson about "a party of negroes and Indians" that Georgia's governor reported were gathering on the river near the Florida border. "It would perhaps be advisable not to remove all the troops from that post," he wrote, referring to Fort Scott."[1]

Such concerns were magnified in January when news reached Georgia's capital city of Milledgeville that Maj. George Woodbine, former second-in-command to Lt. Col. Edward Nicolls, was back in Florida:

> Mr. Kingsley of East Florida has this day informed me that Woodbine has returned to Bowlegs Town at Swaney and has been telling the Negroes that freedom had been granted the blacks at the neighboring Islands; that theirs

> was withheld by the villany of the white people – this he was told at St. Augustine last week by Mr. Popall and by Mr. Dexter. – at Swaney there are (he says) a great many run-away negroes from Georgia who receive and protect all that go to them, and prevent all those that wish to return to their masters from doing so. All those belonging to Mr. Popall and the most part of his wished to return, but were hindered by them from doing so. – He says that it is reported that Woodbine has gone to Havanah and left a white man there as an agent until his return. This information I conceived it to be my duty to make known to your excellency without delay.[2]

Gov. David B. Mitchell relayed the information to Secretary Graham without delay. The governor had already protested the removal of the 4th Infantry from Georgia and now reiterated his concerns in letters to both the Secretary and Gen. Gaines. A return to Florida by Nicolls or Woodbine was a matter of great alarm to residents of the frontier and such rumors were sometimes disproved by subsequent events. On this occasion, however, there was some truth behind the alarm. Woodbine, no longer a British officer, was engaged in a shadowy plot to seize some or all of Florida from Spain. The identity of the agent or assistant left behind at Suwannee is not known, but it was probably either Alexander Arbuthnot or former Lt. Robert Ambrister of the Colonial Marines. Both men became involved in the affairs of the Seminoles and Red Sticks. "I think the information communicated may be relied upon as true," Mitchell wrote, "and furnishes a strong additional reason against the removal of the troops."[3]

The evacuation of Fort Scott also raised concerns across the line in Spanish Florida. John Forbes & Company had reestablished its trading post at Prospect Bluff following the destruction of the Negro Fort. The departure of the troops from the lower Flint led to a surge in threats against company employee Edmund Doyle who had been assigned to rebuild the store:

> ...Since the evacuation of the Camp on Flint River we have had very trying times here. I never suffered more uneasiness from various sources. I think now everything is safe and we shall have quiet times in the Nation: On the 23rd Inst four negroes came here from the Mikasukkys and demanded of me protection which of course was offered; they returned same day to bring the rest of their party there, they belong to a Mr. Kingsley of St. John's River.[4]

Doyle's hope that tensions were calming proved to be premature. Within days of his report a large force of Red Stick warriors arrived at Fort Scott with torches in hand. Lt. Richard Sands was in command of the garrison at Fort Gaines when a courier arrived from down the Chattahoochee:

> When the colonel with the troops left Fort Scott, he gave the buildings in charge of one of the Perrymans, from whom I have just received a letter, handed me by his brother, who arrived here after I had commenced writing this.
>
> Perryman states in his letter that the Red Sticks, (or hostiles) after we had left the fort, came in companies and carried off every thing we had left with him, and what he had purchased of Butler; burnt three houses, and threatened, if he did not leave the place, to burn it over his head. He got what few articles he could, with his family, in a canoe, and came to his brother's, who informs me that there are at present about 300 Indians embodied at the forks, and others constantly joining them. He does not know their intentions, but understood a party was going out to steal horses &c. &c.[5]

The Perrymans were members of an extensive mestizo family that lived along the lower Chattahoochee River. The progeny of the English trader

Theophilus Perryman, they included William, George, Ben and others. Another member of the large family, Thomas Perryman, had been an important leader of the Lower Creek/Seminole towns on the Apalachicola and lower Chattahoochee Rivers and a colonel of British auxiliaries during both the American Revolution and War of 1812. He was the father-in-law of the noted adventurer and pirate William Augustus Bowles. He had died in the years following the War of 1812 and William Perryman, himself a captain in the British auxiliaries during the American Revolution and War of 1812, ascended to the leadership of the primary Perryman towns in today's Seminole County, Georgia, and Jackson County, Florida.

William Perryman was the brother of George Perryman, the caretake left behind at Fort Scott and it was to him that George fled with his family following the Red Stick attack. William carried news of the partial burning of Fort Scott up to Fort Gaines where he met with Lt. Sands and discussed the growing turbulence in the borderlands. The Red Sticks were not far behind and by the next morning had made their presence known:

> This morning [February 3, 1817] one of the settlers waited on me to advise in what manner to act, as eight or ten Indians had been at his house and ordered him off; telling him that in six days they would come back, and, if he was not gone, they would drive him away.
>
> Let their intentions be what they will I feel perfectly safe with my small command (32) & can contend with safety against 500 Indians if we had but five minutes notice of their approach. I have three 5 8/10 inch Howitzers, 2 Sixes & 1 four pounder and ammunition in abundance.[6]

General Gaines was then in Milledgeville where on February 5th he learned from Gov. Mitchell of a raid by a different group in Wayne County, Georgia. A party of warriors had entered the county and stolen two horses and a few head of cattle. Local residents pursued them but the raiders "immediately fired upon the whites, who retired without returning a shot." One of the whites was mortally wounded.[7]

The general promised "immediate and particular" attention:

> ...I am not authorized to change the destination of the 4th infantry; but, should I receive no authority to recall a part of that corps, I shall order one or two companies of artillery (to do duty as infantry) from Charleston to the southern frontier of this State, with instructions to check Indian hostilities, and at the same time to remove from Indian land such intruders as may remain after being duly notified to remove.[8]

Until troops could make the long journey back to Flint River, Fort Gaines was the only U.S. military stronghold against incursions from the Florida frontier between the St. Mary's River and Fort Crawford north of Pensacola. The border stretched for hundreds of miles between the two points and there was little the single company at Fort Gaines could do but watch over the Chattahoochee River and protect the immediate vicinity of the post. Gaines was referring to the frontier village growing around the fort when he reported that the Red Sticks had "given some recent indications of a hostile disposition towards the little settlement upon the Chattahoochie."[9]

Gen.Gaines also notified Gov. Mitchell of the developing situation on the frontier, suggesting that militia troops be called out to protect against any eventuality. Mitchell responded on February 16th with news that "as of yet I do not feel authorized to order out any militia," although he did feel that militia troops would soon be available to "punish the Seminolies." He doubted they could be mustered and placed into the field before the "expected conflict at Pensacola will either have taken place or become as less probable than at present." The references was to a rumored attempt by anti-Spanish adventurers to seize the West Florida city.[10]

The leaders of the filibuster attempt tried to obtain arms from the U.S. military but were refused. This caused their plan to wither on the vine and no attack against Pensacola took place. There was plenty of tension elsewhere, particularly on the lower Chattahoochee River. George Perryman, the former caretaker, wrote to Lt. Sands on February 24th to provide new information about what was happening on the frontier below. The following excerpts have been edited for clarity:

> ...There was a friend of mine not long since in the lower town on Flint [i.e. Fowltown] & he saw many horses, cattle and hogs that had came immediately from the State [of] Georgia and they are bringing them away continually. They speak in the most contemptuous manner of Americans and threat to have satisfaction for what has been done, meaning the destruction of the Negro fort. There is another of my acquaintances returned immediately from the Seminolie Towns, and saw the negroes there on parade. He counted about six hundred that bore arms. They have chosen officers of every description and endeavor to keep up a regular discipline and is very strict in punishing violators of their Military orders.[11]

The Perrymans were former allies of the alliance of Seminole and Red Stick towns and maintained many contacts with them. This allowed them to provide a great deal of intelligence to U.S. authorities. Kenhajo [Cappachimico] of Miccosukee was resisting war, but otherwise the talk among the Seminoles and Red Sticks was for conflict with either "the Americans or McIntosh's troops." Perryman informed Sands that the warriors were promising a much more severe fight for U.S. forces "than they had at Appalachicola."[12]

The former caretaker also reported the growing role of a chief named Boleck (or Bowlegs). He was a leader of the Alachua Seminoles who had been driven from his home by American forces during a brief invasion of East Florida. Boleck's town was destroyed and his brother, Payne, was killed in battle with the Americans. The infuriated chief relocated to the Suwannee where he joined the alliance assembled by Lt. Col. Edward Nicolls and Maj. George Woodbine in 1814-1815. The destruction of the fort at Prospect Bluff deprived him of his primary source for arms and ammunition, but the arrival of a Scottish trader named Alexander Arbuthnot on the Suwannee allowed him to replenish his supply.

The Red Sticks and many of the Seminoles now chose him as their leader/ Perryman reported that they had nominated him king and were paying him "all kind of Monarchial Respect almost to Idolatry." They also kept pickets out at distances of five miles from their towns.[13]

Perryman's account provided an extremely rare contemporary glimpse of the activities taking place at the Seminole and maroon towns on the Suwannee River. These towns were located at present-day Old Town in Dixie County, Florida. Boleck's people lived separately but shared their fields and many resources with a village of several hundred maroons. Many of the men from the latter community had served in Nicolls' Colonial Marines and were well trained in light infantry tactics. Their presence in growing numbers on the Suwannee almost immediately replaced the fort at Prospect Bluff as a point of fixation in the minds of U.S. slave holders.

Hostility on the frontier continued to worsen. A party of warriors struck the Garrett farm in Camden County, Georgia, on the same day as Perryman's letter from the lower Chattahoochee:

> On the 24th instant the house of Mr. Garrett, residing in the upper part of this county, near the boundary of Wayne Co. was attacked, during his absence near the middle of the day, by this party consisting of about fifteen, who shot Mrs. Garrett in two places, and then dispatched her by stabbing and scalping. Her two children, one about three years & the other two months, were also murdered, and the eldest scalped; the house was then plundered of every article of value, and set on fire – a young man in the neighbourhood at work hearing the report of guns went immediately towards the house where he discovered the murdered family. The family having only commenced were soon extinguished – and he spread the alarm.[14]

Archibald Clark, the Intendant of St. Marys and author of the above, reported that workmen from his mills assembled with a few others of the neighborhood assembled to give pursuit but they had few arms. They followed the tracks of the raiding party down the western branch of Spanish Creek but soon gave up the chase. Clark pleased for help in a letter to Milledgeville.[15]

Clark believed that the warriors were "Lower Creeks," but others later blamed Miccosukees for the attack. The murders heightened tensions on the frontier but it was a letter that arrived at Fort Gaines a few days later that sent them soaring. Datelined from Okolokne (Ochlockonee) Sound, the missive was signed by Alexander Arbuthnot who claimed to be representing the Red Stick chief Peter McQueen:

> When McQueen left Tucky Batche his property was considerable both in negroes and cattle; of the former, ten grown negroes were taken by a half breed man named Barney, nine of which he believes were sold & one a girl is still in possession of said Barney: Twenty able negroes were taken by a Chief named Colonel, or Auche Hatcho – who acts also as an interpreter; and as he never had possession of any of those persons' property, nor ever did them an injury to his knowledge; he claims as farther proof of your friendship, that you will use your influence in procuring those Negroes for them; And, should they be given up by the persons holding them, there is one faithful Negro among them named Charles who will bring them to him at Okolockne River.[16]

Arbuthnot described McQueen as "an unfortunate Indian chief" who had been forced to flee his home at Tuckabatchee during the Creek War of 1813-1814. He sought the help of the military in returning to him an African American man named Joe.

The request stunned U.S. officers and civilians alike. McQueen was a bitter enemy and one of the principal leaders of the Red Stick movement.

The sudden appearance of a new British "agent" in Spanish Florida was even more concerning. The letter from Arbuthnot confirmed rumors of a renewed British presence among the Seminoles and Red Sticks. The Americans recognized that the Scottish trader appeared to be speaking on behalf of the Indians in a manner that far exceeded those of a businessman. The document also included a claim that an important British official was on his way:

> I hold in my possession a letter received from the Governor of New Providence, addressed to him by His Britannic Majesty's chief secretary, informing of the orders given to the British ambassador at Washington to watch over the interests of the Indian nations, and see that their rights are faithfully attended to and protected, agreeably to the treaty of peace made between the British and Americans.
>
> I am in hopes that ere this there is arrived at New Providence a person from Great Britain with authority to act as agent for the Indian nations; and, if so, it will devolve on him to see that boundary lines, as marked out by the treaty, are not infringed upon.[17]

Such statements did not go over well in the United States. The letter was similar to ones that Lt. Col. Nicolls had sent to Col. Benjamin Hawkins following the end of the War of 1812. The very thought of British agents on the border was enough to inspire the ire of military commanders such as Andrew Jackson and Edmund P. Gaines.

More information came on March 15, 1817, when Lt. Sands informed Col. William King of the 4th Infantry that William Perryman had arrived at Fort Gaines with reports that a British force was coming to the Gulf Coast:

> ...Yesterday, William Perryman, accompanied by two of the lower chiefs, arrived here. He informs me that McQueen, the chief mentioned in one of the enclosed

> letters, is at present one of the heads of the hostiles; that they are anxious for war, and have lately murdered a woman and two children.
>
> He likewise says he expects the news in George Perryman's letter is true; for there are talks going through the towns that the English are to be at Ochlochnee river in three months.
>
> I have sent an Indian runner to Ochlochnee to ascertain what preparations the hostiles are making.[18]

Gaines had heard enough. Obtaining authority from Maj. Gen. Jackson, he dispatched orders on March 24th for a company of artillery to move from Charleston to Fort Scott. The Federal contractor in Georgia was told in no uncertain terms to begin delivering rations to Chattahoochee:

> You are hereby required to keep up a supply of rations for one hundred men at Fort Scott near the confluence of Flint and Chatahoochie rivers, for Four Months always in advance. This supply to consist of Flour and Bacon or such Pickled Pork as may have been preserved for safe keeping through the summer, together with the small parts of the ration required by the contract – the whole to be kept in store, independent of the casual supplies of fresh beef &c., depending upon the thing settlements in the vicinity of that post. The above supply for the first four months maybe deposited and issued at Fort Gaines, until ordered by the Commanding Officer at that Post to Fort Scott.[19]

Gaines told the contractor that the troops from Charleston could escort the first shipment of provisions as they passed from Fort Hawkins down to the frontier.

The general believed that attacks against the frontier were coming and that Fort Gaines would be a target. He told Lt. Sands to be on the alert for any danger and to summon the settlers of the neighborhood into the fort where the men could assist in its defense and the women and children would be safe under the protection of its guns. He promised Sands that Maj. William McIntosh would be sent down from Coweta with some of his best warriors if the situation became critical. The lieutenant, meanwhile, was to prepare boats to help the artillery company reach Fort Scott.[20]

Troubling reports continued to reach officials in Georgia. One came from Timothy Barnard, a trader who had married a Yuchi woman and lived with his extensive family on the Flint River. He reported on March 29th that the Red Sticks were dancing the "Dance of the Indians of the Lakes," a reference to the old war dance learned in the days before the Creek War of 1813-1814. He went on to report that the evacuation of Fort Scott had convinced the warriors that the troops of the United States were afraid to continue there.

Governor Mitchell, the recipient of Barnard's letter, had resigned his office on the March 4, 1817 to become the new Agent for Indian Affairs. Long-time agent Col. Benjamin Hawkins had died in 1816 and his duties were now entrusted to Mitchell. He informed the Secretary of War that Timothy Barnard had lived among the Creeks for more than 50 years and was extremely well-informed due to this long residence and his many family connections. Barnard's account, he reported, was supported by others from the frontier:

> As an additional inducement to this measure, I will further state that I have received information from other persons at or near Fort Gaines that a British agent is now among these hostile Indians, and that he has been sending insolent messages to the friendly Indians and white men settled above the Spanish line: he is also charged with stimulating the Indians to their present hostile aspect; but whether he is an acknowledged agent of any foreign Power, or a mere adventurer, I do not pretend to determine, but am disposed to believe him the latter; but, be that as it may, and let the hostile disposition of the Indians proceed from what it may, a moderate regular force stationed at Camp

> Crawford, or any other suitable position in that quarter, will, I am confident, keep all quiet; and, without it, some serious mischief will result.[21]

Gaines, meanwhile, was back at Camp Montgomery, Alabama, on April 2, 1817, from where he informed Andrew Jackson that the Red Stick looting of Fort Scott had been confirmed as had the burning of the new barracks there. The general gave the the latest information on the Garrett attack and then addressed the presence of Alexander Arbuthnot in Spanish Florida, whom he labeled "one of those self-styled Philanthropists who have long infested our neighboring Indian villages, in the character of British Agents." He went on to accuse Arbuthnot of "fomenting a spirit of discord" that would lead to the "destruction of these wretched savages."[22]

The general also asked Maj. William McIntosh to take a company of his best warriors down to Fort Gaines. He informed Lt. Sands of this in a letter that urged him to "store up every bushel of corn and every pint of meat you can obtain." War was on the horizon:

> If you should have war your command will be a perilous one; but I am sure it will not on that account be the less desirable to you. He who would woo the sweet goddess of Military fame, must calculate upon finding her only in the midst of dangers.[23]

On the same day, April 2, 1817, Gaines received a letter from a settler named Alexander McCulloh who was living near Fort Gaines. The document was undated but had been written sometime in March. McCulloh, whose name is sometimes given incorrectly as Culloh, told the general that he and other settlers had gathered under the safety of the cannon of Fort Gaines and were unable to make a crop or safely evacuate to a more populated area:

> We are hourly told, by every source of information, by the friendly Indians, by letters from Wm. Hambly and

> Edmund Doyle, who resides low down on the Appalachicola, that all the lower tribes of Indians are embodied, and are drying their meats to come on to the attack of this post. The British agent at Oakclocking Sound is giving presents to the Indians. We have amongst us Indians who have been down and received powder, lead, tomahawks, knives, and a drum for each town, with the Royal Coat-of-Arms painted on it. We have, at this time, at least five hundred Indians skulking in this neighborhood, within three or four miles of us, who will not act for themselves and who are evidently waiting the signal to strike an effectual blow. They have stolen almost every horse belonging to the citizens, they have scared them from the fields which they have cleared and have taken possession of their houses.[24]

McCulloh begged Gaines to send more troops as a strong force was the only way to protect the frontier and its residents. The general responded two weeks later by ordering the commanding officer at Charleston to detach another company of artillery and move it down the coast by water to St. Marys. The troops were to go up the St. Marys River to Camp Pinckney and build a small fort with two blockhouses for the protection of Camden and Wayne Counties. The artillerymen were to carry muskets and bayonets so they could serve as infantry, but were also instructed to carry two 6-pounder field guns to their new post. The captain of the company was also to "take the most effectual measures in his power to protect the defenceless inhabitants from Indian depredation" and was to arrest or destroy "any hostile party of Indians found lurking about that frontier."[25]

Captain Sanders Donoho's company from the 4th Artillery reached Fort Gaines on its way from Charleston to Fort Scott during the late spring of 1817. The unit halted only briefly before moving on in early June to its new posting on the Flint. Donoho reported on June 23 that he had Fort Scott "in a state of defence capable of repelling a thousand Indians, with the force under my command." Although he reported that he was ready for a fight, he also expressed a belief that the fort would not be attacked:

> ...[F]rom all the information I have been able to collect respecting the intentions of the lower creeks, they seem to me to be more disposed to massacre and plunder the defenceless and helpless, than to attack military posts. For the purpose however of ascertaining their final intentions, I despatched an Indian into Florida, whose report as soon as he returns, shall be communicated to you.
>
> I am sorry to inform you that what with desertions, and discharges that are soon to take place, I shall scarcely have an artificer left.[26]

The reoccupation of Fort Scott provided an additional point of defense on the frontier and lessened the tension some at Fort Gaines, at least for the moment.

---

[1] Hon. George Graham to Maj. Gen. Andrew Jackson, November 5, 1816, Library of Congress.
[2] William Gibson to Gov. David B. Mitchell, January 4, 1817, Andrew Jackson Papers, Library of Congress.
[3] Gov. David B. Mitchell to George Graham, Acting Secretary of War, January 13, 1817, Andrew Jackson Papers, Library of Congress.
[4] Edmund Doyle to John Innerarity, January 28, 1817; FHQ, XVIII, October 1939, No. 2. pp. 312-313.
[5] Lt. Richard M. Sands to Commanding Officer Fort Hawkins, February 2, 1817, Andrew Jackson Papers, Library of Congress.
[6] *Ibid.*
[7] Gov. David B. Mitchell to Maj. Gen. Edmund P. Gaines, February 5, 1817, *American State Papers*, Indian Affairs, Volume II, p. 155.
[8] Maj. Gen. Edmund P. Gaines to Gov. David B. Mitchell, February 5, 1817, *American State Papers*, Indian Affairs, Volume II, p. 155.
[9] *Ibid.*

[10] Gov. David B. Mitchell to Maj. Gen. Edmund P. Gaines, February 16, 1817, Adjutant General, Letters Received, NARA.
[11] George Perryman to Lt. Richard M. Sands, February 24, 1816, Andrew Jackson Papers, Library of Congress. Edited for clarity by the author.
[12] *Ibid.*
[13] *Ibid.*
[14] Archibald Clark to Maj. Gen. Edmund P. Gaines, February 26, 1817, Andrew Jackson Papers, Library of Congress. (Similar letter sent to Hon. David B. Mitchell, Agent for Indian Affairs, on the same date.)
[15] *Ibid.*
[16] Alexander Arbuthnot to the Officer Commanding at Fort Gaines, March 3, 1817, Andrew Jackson Papers, Library of Congress.
[17] *Ibid.*
[18] Lt. Richard M. Sands to Col. William King, March 15, 1817, *American State Papers*, Indian Affairs, Volume II, p. 156.
[19] Maj. Gen. Edmund P. Gaines to the Contractor for the State of Georgia, March 24, 1817, Andrew Jackson Papers, Library of Congress.
[20] Maj. Gen. Edmund P. Gaines to Lt. Richard M. Sands, March 26, 1817, Andrew Jackson Papers, Library of Congress.
[21] Hon. David B. Mitchell to the Secretary of War, March 30, 1817, *American State Papers*, Indian Affairs, Volume II, pp. 156-157.
[22] Maj. Gen. Edmund P. Gaines to Maj. Gen. Andrew Jackson, April 2, 1817.
[23] Maj. Gen. Edmund P. Gaines to Lt. Richard M. Sands, April 2, 1817, Andrew Jackson Papers, Library of Congress.
[24] Alexander McCulloh to Maj. Gen. Edmund P. Gaines, n.d. (apparently late March 1817 and received at Camp Montgomery on April 2, 1817), Andrew Jackson Papers, Library of Congress. An edited version of this letter has appeared in numerous print sources incorrectly giving McCulloh's name as "A. Culloh" and with numerous other transcription errors.
[25] Maj. Gen. Edmund P. Gaines to Commanding Officer, Harbor of Charleston, April 16, 1817, Office of the Adjutant General, Letters Received, 1805-1821.
[26] Capt. Sanders Donoho to Maj. Gen. Edmund P. Gaines, June 23, 1817, Andrew Jackson papers, Library of Congress.

CHAPTER SIX

Tensions on the Georgia Frontier

The situation on the frontier convinced military planners that additional troops would be needed at Forts Gaines and Scott and that better roads would be needed to link key military posts. To help achieve these aims, a company of 73 men from the 7th Infantry started overland from Fort Crawford under Maj. David E. Twiggs. The men were ordered to mark paths for new wagon roads that would link Fort Crawford with Fort Gaines and then Fort Gaines with Fort Scott. Twiggs was to take command of the latter post upon his arrival there.

Major Twiggs, nicknamed the "Bengal Tiger," was a particularly stern disciplinarian. A veteran of the War of 1812 he was 27 years old at the time of his march through the South Alabama wilderness. His men were exposed to rain on each day of their journey, a condition that turned the march into a miserable slog through water and mud. They built blockhouses at key crossings of the Yellow Water and Choctawhatchee Rivers, leaving a miniscule force of one corporal and four privates at each place. The men were far away from support of any kind and the blockhouses entrusted to their protection must have been very strong. Twiggs estimated that the total distance from Fort Crawford to Fort Gaines was around 130 miles and reported that it would take 100 soldiers on pioneer duty one month to build a useable road along his route of march.[1]

Twiggs and his command reached Fort Gaines on June 29, 1817. They halted there to rest for a couple of days following a march that the major described as particularly grueling;

> We arrived here late last evening being detained on the way by our horses, a number gave out and we had to leave some that were not able to carry the pack saddles, in fact there are not more than three or four fit for service, their backs with all the attention we could bestow are the worst I ever saw. I shall take them to Fort Scott where I shall be able probably to have them restored in a few weeks. We had rain every day since we left Conaka.[2]

The company moved on from Fort Gaines by boat on July 1, dropping down the Chattahoochee River to its new post on the Flint. Fort Gaines by then had only forty days of flour rations on hand. Beef, fortunately, was available "in almost any quantity" and the Seminoles and Red Sticks had been quiet for the last several weeks.[3]

Gen. Gaines now moved forward with plans to build a military road along Twiggs' path from Fort Crawford to Fort Gaines. This would improve communication between the two posts and ease the progress of the full bodies of the 4th and 7th regiments as they marched from Camps Montgomery and Montpelier to Fort Scott. The general believed that the two regiments would give him sufficient firepower to defeat the Seminoles and Red Sticks near the Apalachicola, but warned Gov. William Rabun of Georgia that he would need more men if Gen. Jackson continued to insist on the capture of the warriors responsible for the Garrett murders:

> ...I have ascertained that a strong spirit of hostility towards us still exists among them; I have therefore made arrangements for assembling at Fort Scott, near the head of the Appalachicola river, in next month, the whole of my disposable force, in order to settle our differences with the Indians, and put a stop to the predatory war, carried on for

> some time past at the expense of the lives and property of unoffending and helpless settlers.[4]

Gaines asked Gov. Rabun to call out one battalion of riflemen and another of light infantry or mounted infantry with orders to be ready to assemble at Fort Hawkins in August for two months' service. The men were to be armed, clothed and equipped. Supplies for operations on the frontier were being sent via the Gulf of Mexico:

> I have ordered a supply of provisions and other military stores to the Appalachicola by water, to be delivered at Fort Scott by the 30th of next month – at which time I wish to be in readiness to adjust our difference with the Indians. – Should they be disposed to continue in a state of war, they shall receive a full portion of its evils; but, should they desire peace, and yield to the demands of justice, they shall be gratified. In this case the troops will be occupied in completing a road which I have commenced from this place, via Fort Crawford on the Conaka, to cross the Chattahoochie about midway between Forts Scott and Gaines, and thence to Hartford in Georgia. – By this route the distance from Georgia to this place and Mobile will be considerably shortened.[5]

Gaines' request did not reach Milledgeville for two full months and by the Rabun received it the rendezvous time for the militia had already passed. The governor did what he could by ordering the men of Irwin's Blackshear's, Hamilton's and Scott's Brigades to be ready on a moment's notice.[6]

A council at Fort Scott on August 4 failed to ease tensions on the Spanish border. Maj. Gen. Gaines now informed Jackson that "nothing but the application of force, will be sufficient to ensure a permanent adjustment of this affair." He was ordering the movement of the 4th and 7th Infantry regiments to Fort Scott and believed that they would be on the Flint by the

20th or 25th of October. Heavy supplies were being sent by water under military escort and the new road across the ceded lands in South Alabama was being finished.[7]

Gov. Rabun moved into action by ordering a squadron of cavalry and ten companies of infantry to be ready to march on short notice from their home counties of Hancock, Washington, Baldwin, Putnam, Morgan, Twiggs, Pulaski, Jones and Jasper. Arms and accoutrements would be provided for them at Fort Hawkins. The *Georgia Journal* in Milledgeville reported, however, that the troops would probably not be needed:

> We learn by a gentleman from Head Quarters, (Fort Montgomery) that Gen. Gaines, who was then at St. Stephens, intends visiting Georgia in a few days; and that but little expectation appeared to be entertained in that part of the country, of an approaching rupture with the Indians. It is probable, therefore, the troops from this State will not be called into service.[8]

The soldiers of the 4th and 7th Infantry Regiments probably knew that they were marching into a hornets' nest. The Fowltown chief Neamathla (Eneah Emathla) had made clear that he would not be driven from his lands. He had not been party to the Treaty of Fort Jackson and did not consider himself to be bound by it. No sooner had Donoho and Twiggs reached Fort Scott than did the chief warn them not to cut timber on his side of the Flint River. He met with Maj. Twiggs on August 3, 1817, to warn that he would oppose by force any American effort to take his lands:

> ... the Chief of Fowl town near this who is very frequently among the Seminolas told me eight days ago that the Flint river was the line between us & I must not cut another stick of timber on the opposite side from this, the land was his & he was directed by the Powers above to protect & defend it & he should do so & I would see that talking could not frighten him since which I have not seen one of his town.

> The Indians on the east of the Flint will in my opinion in the event of a movement on that side of the river commence hostilities. It is possible I may be mistaken but I shall think so till the contrary is proved.[9]

The public contractor in Georgia, meanwhile, failed to deliver expected supplies to either Fort Scott or Fort Gaines. The stocks of provisions at both forts were dwindling and Maj. Twiggs notified Gen. Gaines on the 11th that he had been forced to evacuate the blockhouse on the Choctawhatchee because Lt. Sands at Fort Gaines could no longer supply the five men there. The blockhouse on the Yellow Water was probably being supplied through Fort Crawford and Twiggs made no mention of its fate.[10]

Let down by the contractor, Army officers turned to the Pensacola firm of John Forbes & Company for help in getting provisions to Fort Scott and Fort Gaines. Storekeeper Edmund Doyle reported from Prospect Bluff on August 17th that 125,000 rations ordered by Gen. Gaines were either at the bluff or on their way up to the forts. Another 125,000 rations were still expected. He also requested more goods and noted that he was buying corn for the sutler at Fort Scott at a price of no more than 6 reals per bushel. In Spanish silver coinage, this was about the equivalent of 75 cents. He had also sold the sutler $190 worth of sugar and coffee at 19 and 17 cents per pound respectively.[11]

Acting Secretary of War George Graham approved the march of the 4th and 7th Infantries to the region of the lower Chattahoochee and Flint rivers on October 30, 1817:

> ...I am instructed by [the President] to inform you that he approves of the movement of the troops from Fort Montgomery to Fort Scott. The appearance of this additional force, he flatters himself, will at least have the effect of restraining the Seminoles from committing further depredations, and, perhaps, of inducing them to make reparation for the murders which they have committed.

> Should they, however, persevere in their refusal to make such reparation, it is the wish of the President that you should not on that account pass the line and make an attack upon them within the limits of Florida, until you shall have received instructions from this Department.[12]

The orders were an authorization for war. This was made even more clear by the second part of the Secretary's letter, which gave Gen. Gaines approval for movements to expel such villages as Fowltown from the ceded lands:

> You are authorized to remove the Indians still remaining on the lands ceded by the treaty made by General Jackson with the Creeks; and, in doing so, it may be proper to retain some of them as hostages until reparation may have been made for the depredations which have been committed. McIntosh and the other chiefs of the Creek nation, who were here some time since, expressed then, decidedly, their unwillingness to permit any of the hostile Indians to return to their nation.[13]

Graham cautioned Gaines not to disturb any Creeks with claims to reservations of land under the provisions of the Treaty of Fort Jackson. His authorization to take hostages, however, was particularly blunt. Whether he understood the "eye for an eye" culture of the Creek and Seminole Indians is not clear.[14]

The Creeks and Seminoles also recognized that war was imminent. Rumors reached the American posts in late September that a mass meeting of chiefs and warriors had been held at Miccosukee:

> ...I have a character in confinement, who was present at the meeting at the Mikasuka town the last of September. The determination of the Indians is, to give up no murderers or others to the whites, and as soon as we cross Flint River to

> attack us. The chiefs counted the number present at the meeting – there were 2700 warriors."[15]

General Gaines and other U.S. officers would question the claim that the Seminoles and Red Sticks could muster 2,700 warriors, but the number was consistent with British reports of the strength of their allies on the Apalachicola during the War of 1812. Twiggs believed that troops would be attacked as soon as they crossed the Flint River.

Gaines reacted to this latest report with a direct message to the chiefs and warriors aligned to oppose the United States:

> The president of the United States has been informed of the murders and thefts committed by the hostile Indians in this part of the country. He has authorized General Jackson to arrest the offenders, and cause justice to be done. The Indians have been required to deliver up the murderers of our citizens, and the stolen property, but they refused to deliver either; they have had a council at Mickasukee, in which they determined upon war; they have been at war against helpless women and children, let them now calculate upon fighting men.[16]

The general explained that he knew the United States had enemies across the Flint, but also tried to reassure friendly towns that no harm would come to them.. "The President," he wrote, "wishing to do justice to his red friends and children, has given orders for the bad to be separated from the good." He challenged the bands for war against the United States to assemble at Miccosukee and Suwannee while at the same time urging those who wished peace to stay home and help supply the army. He then alluded to rumors that the British were coming to join the fray:

> ...The hostile party pretend to calculate upon help from the British! They may as well look for soldiers from the moon to help them. Their warriors were beaten, and driven from

> our country by American troops. The English are not able to help themselves: how, then, should they help the old "Red Sticks," whom they have ruined by pretended friendship?[17]

As these communications were taking place, U.S. troops were on the move. Gen. Gaines led the main bodies of the 4th and 7th Infantries in person from their barracks and along the long march on the new road from Fort Crawford to Fort Gaines. The troops left Camp Montgomery on October 27, 1817, and reached Fort Gaines on November 9th. It was the second time that Gaines had visited the fort that bore his name. He reported to Gen. Jackson from there that he had learned of the presence of 35 Yuchi warriors near the mouth of the Yellow Water River in wester Florida. Among them were believed to be some of the murderers Johnson and McGaskey as well as the killer of a third man named Mr. Glass who had been slain near Murder Creek in Southwest Alabama. The band had stolen some horses and "declared their determination to be always hostile towards our citizens."[18]

Gaines did not know it, but even as he filed his report to Jackson from Fort Gaines, the Monroe Administration in Washington, D.C. was allowing other events to assume greater importance than the looming war with the Red Stick Creeks and Seminoles. Secretary Graham wrote to the general on November 12th to order him to immediately leave for a new front:

> I am instructed by the President to direct you to repair immediately to Point Petre. The enclosed copies of letters addressed to Lt. Colo. Bankhead and to the Governor of Georgia, will advise you of the object of this order, and the necessity of a prompt execution of it.
>
> If previously to reaching point Petre, you should be advised of the abandonment, or surrender of Amelia Island, you will then exercise your discretion as to the point which you may select for your Head Quarters.[19]

Sudden events at Amelia Island had drawn the full attention of authorities in Washington, D.C. The enigmatic Scottish-born soldier of fortune Gregor MacGregor appeared off Fernandina in June 1817 and took the town and island from the Spanish. Supposedly commissioned by the South American revolutionary Simon Bolivar, MacGregor raised the Green Cross of Florida flag and declared that he had revolutionized Spain's Florida colonies. The adventurer's dream of taking all of East and West Florida fizzled, however, and he sailed away for new adventures in September. The pirate/privateer Louis-Michel Aury (usually called Luis Aury) then took control of the island in the name of the Republic of Mexico.

The United States was not thrilled with this turmoil and the Monroe Administration ordered U.S. troops to seize Amelia Island. Gen. Gaines was to lead them, but would not learn of his orders until another war had exploded around him on the Georgia frontier.

---

[1] Maj. David E. Twiggs to Maj. Gen. Edmund P. Gaines, June 29, 1817, Andrew Jackson Papers, Library of Congress.

[2] *Ibid.*

[3] *Ibid.*

[4] Maj. Gen. Edmund P. Gaines to the Governor of Georgia, July 20, 1817, included in Georgia Journal, September 15, 1817.

[5] *Ibid.*

[6] *Ibid.*

[7] Maj. Gen. Edmund P. Gaines to Maj. Gen. Andrew Jackson, October 1, 1817.

[8] *Georgia Journal*, September 30, 1817.

[9] Maj. David E. Twiggs to Hon. David B. Mitchell, August 11, 1817, from the Easton Gazette, April 5, 1819, p. 1.

[10] Maj. David E. Twiggs to Maj. Gen. Edmund P. Gaines, August 11, 1817, Andrew Jackson Papers, Library of Congress.

[11] Edmund Doyle to James Innerarity, August 17, 1817, FHQ, XVIII, October 1939, No. 2, p. 139.

[12] George Graham, Acting Secretary of War, to Maj. Gen. Edmund P. Gaines, October 30, 1817, American State Papers, Indian Affairs, Volume II,

[13] *Ibid.*

[14] *Ibid.*

[15] Maj. David E. Twiggs to Maj. Gen. Edmund P. Gaines, November 1, 1817, appeared in the New York Evening Post, p. 2., December 2, 1817.
[16] Maj. Gen. Edmund P. Gaines to Chiefs and Warriors, November 1817, (Referred to as Enclosure No. 3 in Gaines to Secretary of War, December 2, 1817) ASPMA Vol 1, No. 164. p. 688.
[17] *Ibid.*
[18] Maj. Gen. Edmund P. Gaines to Maj. Gen. Andrew Jackson, November 9, 1817, *American State Papers*, Indian Affairs, Volume II, p. 160.
[19] Hon. George Graham to Maj. Gen. Edmund P. Gaines, November 12, 1817, Adutant General, Letters Received, NARA.

CHAPTER SEVEN

The First Seminole War

General Gaines left Fort Gaines for Fort Scott almost immediately after arriving and took command at the latter post in person in mid-November. The main bodies of the 4th and 7th Regiments trailed behind him, reaching the Chattahoochee River by around November 14, 1817. Lt. Col. Matthew Arbuckle filed the returns for both regiments from a "camp near Fort Gaines" on that date. They did not remain there long as they marched into Fort Scott on the 19th and 20th.[1]

It was likely during this march that the troops built a road that was to have long significance in history of Southwest Georgia. The Three Notch Road, as it is known today, was a wagon road that linked Fort Gaines on the Chattahoochee with Fort Scott on the Flint. Most communication between the two forts prior to November of 1817 had been by water. There was an existing land route via a trail that led down the east side of the Chattahoochee River to Perryman's old town in what is now Seminole County. From there a second trail led east over Spring Creek and to Fort Scott. The new road followed a more direct route and cut numerous miles off the previous route. The name "three notch" supposedly derived from the carving of triple notches into trees along the trail by soldiers to prevent others from losing their way. It is a colorful story that is commonly told throughout the Southeast and there are other Three Notch Roads throughout the region. Early maps of Southwest Georgia show the trail as the "Fort Scott Road." It ran south from Fort Gaines, crossed the modern site of Blakely, then passed near Iron City east of Donalsonville and finally ended at Fort Scott. In 1817, of course, there were no settlements along this road.

It took infantry troops about three days to march the full length of the new road and there is some evidence that breastworks were erected at preselected campsites where each day's march would come to an end. One of these fortifications was located on the north side of Breastwork's Branch in what is now Early County, Georgia, and was shown on the original surveys of the area.

Like the road connecting Fort Gaines with Fort Crawford in Alabama, the new road was more direct but was roughly cut. Larger trees were bypassed and smaller ones were sawed down close to the ground so that wagons could pass over the stumps. Rains would turn the ruts into muddy chasms and it would take years for the passage of feet, hooves and wheels to pack them down and create a more passable road.

The feared war with the Red Sticks and Seminoles erupted less than 48 hours after the troops reached Fort Scott. Gen. Gaines sent Major Twiggs to Fowltown with 250 men and orders to bring Neamathla back to the fort:

> The hostile character & Conduct of the Indians of the Fowl Town, settled within our limits, rendering it absolutely necessary that they should be removed, you will proceed to the town with the detachment assigned you, and remove them. You will arrest and bring the chiefs and warriors to this place, but should they oppose you, or attempt to escape, you will in that event treat them as enemies. Your men are to be strictly prohibited, in any event, from firing upon, or otherwise injuring, women and children.
>
> You will return to this place with your command as soon as practicable.

> Should you receive satisfactory information that any considerable number of the neighboring Indians have joined those of Fowl Town, you will immediately return to this place without making any further attempt to execute first the above written orders.[2]

Twiggs marched on the evening of November 20, 1817, and reached the town during the predawn hours of the next morning. He ordered the companies of Maj. Montgomery and Capt. Birch to move to the right and those of Capts. Allison and Bee to swing to the left while he remained in the center with his own command. The plan was to surround the town and "without blood shed bring to you the chiefs & wariors." Instead, the villages fled from before "the companies of Majr. Montgomery & Cpt. Birch on my right & fired upon my left under Capts. Allison & Bee when they were fired on in return." The first shots of the Seminole Wars had been fired.[3]

Maj. Twiggs failed in his effort to capture Neamathla and returned to Fort Scott emptyhanded except for a few head of cattle. He also brought the unfortunate news that a Creek woman had been killed in the skirmish. Gen. Gaines expressed regret for this loss of life, but had no way of communicating this to the outraged Native Americans who vowed revenge on the U.S. troops for their unprovoked attack.

Lt. Col. Arbuckle was sent back to Fowltown to secure corn from the village's corncribs. He arrived there on November 23, 1817, and was in the process of loading his wagons with looted corn when Neamathla and his warriors attacked. A sharp skirmish resulted and Pvt. Aaron Hughes was killed, as were several Creeks. Hughes was the first U.S. casualty of the Seminole Wars. The warriors withdrew after about 20 minutes of fighting and Arbuckle pulled his men back from the village and marched about three miles to Burges's Bluff on the Flint River. There, where the city of Bainbridge stands today, he built Fort Hughes. The log fort was of almost identical design to Fort Gaines and the lieutenant colonel believed it was closer to that post than Fort Scott, which stood lower down the Flint River:

> The scite of the Fort is on a Bluff sixty or seventy feet above the River and distant about one hundred yards from its edge, the space between the fort and the River and for a considerable distance above and below is very open from this position both on and off the River. There is a considerable portion of good land. The surface of the country is very pleasant and from every appearance must be healthy. This I consider a very advantageous position for a post, it being eight or ten miles nearer to Fort Gaines than [Fort Scott] is and more than that distance nearer to that portion of the Creeks who have commenced the war.[4]

Red Stick and Seminole warriors responded to the U.S. attacks and crossing of the Flint River by sending large parties into the "public lands" to cut off communications between Fort Scott and Fort Gaines. These parties also did their best to half communications between the two forts and he interior posts of Fort Mitchell and Fort Hawkins. The effectiveness of thee war parties was brought home U.S. officials in an alarming way by a courier who tried to make his way from Fort Hawkins to Fort Gaines:

> An express from Gen. Jackson to Gen. Gaines, who left here on Friday, returned to night. He took the route by fort Gaines, but was unable to proceed even that far. He penetrated within ten miles of the fort, where he observed fresh Indian signs; and a few miles further came to where white men had been killed, one of whom was Mr. John Chambers, of fort Gaines.[5]

The courier had gone out apparently not knowing that Gen. Gaines had been ordered from Fort Scott to the St. Marys. He tried to get his message to the general by way of Fort Gaines. He was trailing behind another party of whites and was only five miles away when the attack took place:

> The express had heard from them frequently, by persons whom he met, and was trying to overtake them; and at the time of the murder could not have been more than five miles behind. They were killed last Monday morning, within a few miles of the place where they had encamped the night before. The appearance indicated about twenty Indians, and the trail entered the road in the direction of fort Gaines, at which place there is merely a sergeant's guard of twelve men, and a few of the neighbouring inhabitants, who have taken refuge there. So safe, however, have the inhabitants considered themselves there, that some, it is save, are so credulous as to make their yard railing their only breast-work; and the alarm has come so sudden upon them, that retreat is impossible, or at least dangerous.[6]

The settlers around Fort Gaines once again fled into the stockade. News of the attack led Georgia authorities to order a detachment of militia to the fort with orders to assist in its defense. According to the reminiscences of one of the participants, famed frontiersman Thomas Woodward, the relief party made it through and reached the fort at night. The unidentified officer who relayed word of the situation near Fort Gaines to a Georgia newspaper editor also provided some detail of the military situation on the frontier:

> ,,,Fort Gaines is said to be of considerable strength; fort Scott is a mere camp, having very partial defences. Two expresses dispatched from fort Gaines to fort Scott, have not been heard of; nor has the one sent from this place since he left fort Mitchell. Jackson's express says that he was informed by a friendly chief, that Gen. Gaines had sent advices to fort Mitchell, requesting that as few passages should be made through the nation as possible. This is probably correct and necessary, as the hostile influence seems to be extensive and scattered, and one middle town on the rout to Fort Gaines, which is avowedly hostile, lies

> only thirty-seven miles below the Alabama road. Governor Mitchell is at Fort Mitchell, and will use his influence and authority with the nation in courting their neutrality, or directing their vengeance.[7]

General Thomas Glasscock of the Georgia Militia was at Fort Hawkins with some of his men when the courier arrived. He told the editors of the *Augusta Chronicle* that two men had been killed in the incident, but this news was overshadowed by his report of a much more shocking incident, the destruction of Lt. R.W. Scott's party on the upper Apalachicola River and the deaths of the lieutenant with 34 men, 7 women and 4 children (see Chapter Nine). The general expected to be ordered into combat soon:

> I feel a conscious pride that the small detachment under my command will participate in avenging the death of our slaughtered breathren, as I have no doubt but that gen. Gaines's feelings are sufficiently roused to pursue them to the last extremity, or at least so far as prudence may dictate. I am fearful ere this reaches you, Fort Gaines will fall, and from the success the Indians have lately met with, they will be very bold and daring.[8]

It would take longer than Glasscock hoped to get into action, but he and his men would soon play an important role in American war preparations by advancing to the Flint River and building Fort Early. This post, near present-day Cordele, Georgia, would serve as a key supply depot for U.S. forces being ordered to assemble on the border.

As the war parties hovered around Fort Gaines, occasionally firing on the post, former Gov.David B. Mitchell, now the U.S. Agent for Indian Affairs, attended a council at Broken Arrow. This town was the seat of the Little Prince, principal leader of the Lower Creeks:

> ...[A] meeting of the Principal Chiefs had been called by the Little Prince, at the Town of Thla-Cotch-Cau, on the Chatahoochie River, near Fort Mitchell, at which I attended; the object of which was, to take into consideration the state of the Nation, and particularly, the measures which it would be proper for them to take, in relation to those Indians residing between Fort Gaines and the Spanish Line; and also the conduct they should pursue with regard to the War with the Seminoles. They unanimously expressed much regret, that hostilities should have commenced between the Troops under General Gaines, and the Fowltown Indians, who reside within our Boundary; because these Indians, although they did not unite with the friendly ones during the late War, neither did they join the Red Sticks, and had recently expressed a great desire to become decidedly friendly. They were, however, perfectly willing, that their Warriors should join General Gaines against the Seminoles.[9]

Mitchell told the assembled chiefs that the United States did not want a war with the Seminoles and that he could not approve of Creek warriors crossing the border into Spanish Florida to attack them. He urged them to send a trusted chief to the towns between Fort Gaines and the Spanish line with an urgent appeal that they relocate above the line into the newly defined Creek Nation. This emissary should then go on to Miccosukee to meet with the chiefs there. Once again, the subject of the African Americans living on the Suwannee came into the picture:

> ...[They agreed that] the same Chief should then proceed directly to the Mackasukie Town (the Head-quarters of the Seminoles and Red Sticks of the Late War,) and propose to them certain terms of peace, and a junction of their Force to go against the Negro Camp. The objects which this Chief was instructed to hold out to those Indians, as attainable, by

> adopting this course, were various, and of sufficient importance, in the view of those making the proposition, to induce a belief, that they would be favorably received; in which event I should proceed to Fort Scott to adjust their differences. This course of proceeding was immediately adopted, and the head man of the Osoochies, Hopoi Haijo, set out on the same day, charged with the Mission.[10]

The chiefs felt that it was best to allow this emissary time to meet with the Seminoles and Red Sticks before sending their warriors to assist U.S. forces. They agreed to reconvene on January 11, 1818. Maj. William McIntosh and the warriors would be told to attend with arms and supplies in hand and would march immediately if they were needed to reinforce the army.[11]

Mitchell's efforts to make peace were not received well by U.S. officers at Fort Scott and Fort Gaines. They were under siege and at risk of being either overrun by enemy warriors or forced to evacuate their posts due to provision shortages. They had hoped that McIntosh and his warriors would come down the Chattahoochee to break the siege and help drive back the Seminoles and Red Sticks. Lt. Robert Irvin, now the commanding officer at Fort Gaines, expressed his astonishment that McIntosh was not coming in a report to Lt. Col. Arbuckle at Fort Scott:

> ...[T]he agent had told the Indians that Genl. Gaines had no business to go to the Indian's Town and fire on them in the night, that he had acted like the Indians themselves in doing so – McIntosh had come as far as Fort Mitchell on his way, and the agent has sent him home and told him to meet him at the agency for a Talk in 30 days, 18 of which yet remains, and that he should not move till the general government should give the order. This I expect is the case for they have sent Onos Hadjoe a talk that he was doing wrong to be in service in this country till the agent should give him orders

> – He further states that the agent has sent a talk to Simanola, to the chiefs to meet him and he would make peace for them, and the white people should have no satisfaction for what was done.[12]

The peace council that Mitchell proposed convening at Fort Scott never took place. The arrival of the report on the massacre of Lt. Scott's party in Washington, D.C., ended any restraint on the part of the United States. Orders went out authorizing U.S. troops to cross the line into Spanish Florida to find and punish those responsible. Maj. Gen. Andrew Jackson, the hero of both New Orleans and Horseshoe Bend, was ordered to assemble and army on the frontier and end the threat from below the Spanish border.

General Gaines wrote to Washington as he passed through Georgia on his way to the St. Mary's and his letter offers a good understanding of the American view on why the Seminoles especially had gone to war:

> …The Seminole Indians, however strange and absurd it may appear to those who understand little of their real character and extreme ignorance, entertain a notion that they cannot be beaten by our troops. They confidently assert that we have never beaten them, or any of their people, except when we have been assisted by "red people." This will appear the less extraordinary when it is recollected that they have little or no means of knowing the strength and resources of our country; they have not travelled through it; they read neither books nor newspapers; nor have the opportunities of conversing with persons able to inform them. I feel warranted, from all I know of these savages, in saying that they do not believe we can beat them. This error of theirs has led them, from time to time, for many years past, to massacre our frontier citizens, often the unoffending and helpless mother and babes.[13]

Gaines also explained that he had truly believed that his raids on Fowltown would "be adequate to stop these outrages." He had felt "pleased" with his ability to be "instrumental in effecting an object of so much importance to our exposed frontier settlements." Things had not, he admitted, gone as he expected and he requested permission from Secretary of War Graham to return to Fort Scott.

A hard battle was fought at Ocheesee Bluff on the Apalachicola River in December 1817 but the Seminole War generally remained a conflict of small raids and attacks throughout the winter of 1817-1818. The Native American effort to shut down supply routes to Forts Gaines and Scott proved effective and both garrisons were reduced to the verge of starvation. Lt. Col. Arbuckle warned Gen. Jackson that the situation on the frontier was becoming desperate:

> No provisions has yet reached us. We are now on half rations & have but a few days supply at that rate without a prospect of receiving any more soon.
>
> The contractor's agent left here some time since for Fort Gaines for the purpose of procuring cattle, I have not heard how he has succeeded & fearing that he may not be able to furnish a supply in time, I have ordered Captain Birch with a party of men to repair to Fort Gaines, with a view of collecting cattle or assisting the contractor's agent, in bringing in what he may have collected.[14]

The soldiers at Fort Gaines were slightly better off than those at Fort Scott primarily because they were fewer in number and a few head of cattle could still be obtained from the abandoned farms in the vicinity. This led Lt. Col. Arbuckle, now commanding at Fort Scott, to send troops to secure food from Fort Gaines:

> ...[S]hould Capt. Birch who is now at Fort Gaines, with a command of one hundred and twenty men, for the purpose of obtaining beef, not succeed, and the contractors agents

> persist in neglecting their duty much longer, the consequences must be greatly disastrous to the Troops and Inhabitants of the Chattehooche.[15]

Lt. Col. Arbuckle, almost out of supplies and desperate for help, penned a letter from Fort Scott on February 15, 1818, that earned for him the eternal enmity of many of Andrew Jackson's officers:

> Your express has brought me such information as to alarm me much for the safety of Fort Gaines. He states that about forty miles above this he discovered where at least two hundred Indians had passed in that direction, about three or four days since, and it is unfortunate that we have at this time but twelve or fourteen men at that Post.
>
> If supplies do not arrive here in eight days or there is a certainty by that time of their arriving within a few days after, I shall be compelled to abandon this post with perhaps the whole force, and if Fort Gaines has fallen, that will probably not be the only disaster in this quarter, as the reduction of that Post will much more increase the force of the enemy. Should I be compelled to leave this, I shall march on the west bank of the Flint and endeavor to make Fort Early.[16]

Gen. Gaines was on his way back from the St. Mary's when Arbuckle's dispatch reached him near Hartford, Georgia, on February 20. He immediately shared it with Gen. Jackson. The idea of an American officer abandoning his post in the fact of the enemy ignited an explosion of Jacksonian proportions and close aides of the general would heckle Arbuckle over his threat to flee the Flint River for years to come. Gaines immediately loaded supplies into a boat and set out down the Flint River to stop any move to evacuate Fort Scott. Meanwhile, Lt. Richard M. Sands, former commander of Fort Gaines, arrived in Apalachicola Bay aboard the sloop *Phebe Ann* with a cargo of flour, pork, whiskey and vinegar. He sent news upriver on February 28 that supplies were on the way.[17]

Maj. Enos Cutler, meanwhile, notified Arbuckle on March 1 that he had reached Fort Gaines. Capt. Burch would leave the post the next morning with provisions of beef after having cleared all the cattle on the east side of the Chattahoochee that still had the strength to move. The flight of settlers from their farms into Fort Gaines had left stock with no one to tend for it and the animals were suffering. Cutler also reported that the long expected Creek warriors under Maj. William McIntosh were finally on their way:

> Colo. Brearley writes to me that five hundred Indians are ordered here. They are expected this evening. He directs me to enroll them and to give them orders. I am this day driving up cattle on the other side of the river to give them a little provisions, and shall send them immediately in pursuit of the Red Ground Chief and Mico de coxe.[18]

The Red Ground Chief mentioned in Cutler's report was Econchattimico ("Red Ground King"), the leader of the large Creek town of Ekanachatte on the west bank of the Chattahoochee just below the Alabama line. His warriors had joined in the war against the United States and, fearful of an attack, the chief had withdrawn with his people into the swamps of the upper Chipola River in what is now Jackson County, Florida. "Mico de coxe," meanwhile, was an old chief of long standing in the borderlands. He had allied himself with William Augustus Bowles during that adventurer's second sojourn in Florida.

It took a bit longer for the Creeks to reach Fort Gaines than expected. Maj. McIntosh had been promoted to brigadier general due to the size of the force that he now commanded. He reported from the "Uche Old Fields" between today's cities of Eufaula and Phenix City, Alabama, that his men were experiencing great difficulty due to river and creek flooding. He had already captured three warriors who had been involved in firing on boats on the Apalachicola River. One of them had been wounded in action there, apparently during the Battle of Ocheesee. McIntosh was bringing them to Fort Gaines.[19]

As McIntosh's Creeks continued to work their way down the west side of the Chattahoochee River, Col. A.P. Hayne reached Fort Mitchell on March 2, 1818. He was in command of hundreds of Tennessee Volunteers. Col. David Brearley, the commander of the post, was in a state of great alarm about reports of a lack of supplies downriver. He showed the colonel letters from Fort Scott that contained reports of starvation and hunger. Unsure of what to do, Hayne wrote to Lt. Col. Arbuckle on the same day:

> I have just arrived at this post with the Brigade of Tennessee Volunteers & wish to know whether you will have it your power to feed us, or in other words whether the contemplated supplies of provisions have arrived from New Orleans.
>
> I shall proceed from this place to Fort Gaines where I shall certainly expect to hear from you by express. Our men will draw from this place ten days rations which is all that can be had.
>
> Our route will by way of Fort Perry along the east bank of the Chattahoochee.
>
> I have seen your letter of the 24th of last month & most seriously lament the suffering of the brave troops under your command.
>
> Pray as not fail to let me know whether you can be able to feed us.[20]

Jackson had already ordered Hayne and his Tennesseans to proceed to Fort Scott via Fort Gaines as quickly as possible, but the rumors reaching Fort Mitchell halted them in their tracks. Col. Brearley, unaware that the supply ships expected by Jackson had arrived at Apalachicola, further told Col. Hayne that the expected ships had not been heard from and were feared lost in a storm. Hayne finally decided not to go to Fort Gaines and he had been ordered and instead headed east for the settled areas of Georgia in hopes of finding provisions there. He did not wait to hear back from Arbuckle. The move infuriated Jackson, who could not understand why the Tennesseans would march away from the direction in which supplies were expected to an area that had already been stripped clean of large stocks of food by the passing of Glasscock's Brigade of Georgia Militia. The Tennesseans did not reach Fort Scott until well after Jackson had passed and Col. Brearley would soon face a court martial for his role in the confusion.

The First Seminole War was quickly shifting southward. Andrew Jackson reached Fort Scott with the main body of his army on the night of March 9, 1818, and headed south for Florida on the next day. Despite legend to the contrary, Jackson never visited Fort Gaines. His advance pushed the front of the war out of Southwest Georgia and into Florida, changing Fort Gaines from a frontline defensive post to a supply depot. Before this change took place, however, the fort would play one last major role in the Seminole conflict.

---

[1] Lt. Col. Matthew Arbuckle to Brig. Gen. Daniel Parker, November 14, 1817, Adjutant General, Letters Received, NARA.
[2] Maj. Gen. Edmund P. Gaines to Maj. David E. Twiggs, November 20, 1817, Adjutant General, Letters Received, NARA.
[3] Maj. D.E. Twiggs to Maj. Gen. Edmund P. Gaines, November 21, 1817, Adjutant General, Letters Received, NARA.
[4] Lt. Col. Matthew Arbuckle to Maj. Gen. Edmund P. Gaines, November 30, 1817, Andrew Jackson papers, Library of Congress.
[5] Staff officer to the editor of the Reflector in Milledgeville, December 10, 1817, printed in the Massachusetts Spy, p. 2., December 31, 1817.
[6] *Ibid.*
[7] Staff officer to the editor of the Reflector in Milledgeville, December 10, 1817, printed in the Massachusetts Spy, p. 2., December 31, 1817.
[8] Gen. Thomas Glasscock to the editors of the Augusta Chronicle, December 11, 1817, appeared in the Augusta Chronicle on December 17, 1817.
[9] Hon. David B. Mitchell to Hon. George Graham, Secretary of State, December 14, 1817, British Foreign and State Papers, pp. 1106-1107.

[10] *Ibid.*
[11] *Ibid.*
[12] Lt. Robert Irvin to Lt. Col. Matthew Arbuckle, December 23, 1817, Andrew Jackson papers, Library of Congress.
[13] Maj. Gen. Edmund P. Gaines to Hon. George Graham, Secretary of War, December 15, 1817, American State Papers, Military Affairs, Volume I, p. 689.
[14] *Ibid.*
[15] Lt. Col. Matthew Arbuckle to Maj. Gen. Andrew Jackson, January 12, 1818, Andrew Jackson Papers, Library of Congress.
[16] Lt. Col. Matthew Arbuckle to Maj. Gen. Edmund P. Gaines, February 15, 1818, Adjutant General, Letters Received, NARA.
[17] Lt. R.M. Sands to Lt. Col. Mathew Arbuckle, February 28, 1818, Andrew Jackson Papers, Library of Congress.
[18] Maj. E. Cutler to Lt. Col. Matthew Arbuckle, March 1, 1818, Adjutant General, Letters Received, NARA.
[19] Brig. Gen. William McIntosh to Maj. Daniel Hughes, March 2, 1818, Camden Gazette, April 11, 1818, p. 3.
[20] Col. Arthur P. Hayne to Lt. Col. Matthew Arbuckle, March 2, 1818, Andrew Jackson Papers, Library of Congress.

CHAPTER EIGHT

Warrior Executions at Fort Gaines

The Spring of 1818 was marked by the Chattahoochee River campaign of Brig. Gen. William McIntosh and the U.S. Army's Creek Brigade. A man who truly lived in two worlds, McIntosh was the grandson of a Scottish Highlander, the son of a British military officer and the cousin of George Troup, who served as a U.S. Representative, U.S. Senator and two-term Governor of Georgia. His mother was a Creek woman and he came of age as a warrior and chief in Coweta, the powerful "peace town" of the Creeks. James Floyd, the Principal Chief of the Muscogee (Creek) Nation at the time of this writing, is a descendant of William McIntosh.

The chief and many of his warriors had fought a bitter campaign against the Red Sticks during the Creek War of 1813-1814, saving the life of the Big Warrior but being driven from the Tallapoosa River to the Chattahoochee by overwhelming forces. When the United States entered the fray, they fought side by side with American soldiers to defeat their common enemy. McIntosh played a critical role at the Battle of Horseshoe Bend where he served under Maj. Gen. Andrew Jackson. Promoted to the rank of major, he led Creek forces in the 1816 campaign against the Negro Fort on the Apalachicola. His courage and the performance of his Native American troops during that expedition was praised by Lt. Col. Duncan Clinch.

The forces from Coweta and allied towns now prepared to move against the Red Sticks and Seminoles as part of the massive U.S. mobilization that was underway in the late winter and spring of 1818. With McIntosh at their head, the warriors were ready to once again fight against men from their own Nation at the behest of the United States. They were mustered into the U.S. Army on February 24, 1818, forming a brigade that numbered 1,537 men including officers.

The Creek Brigade left Fort Mitchell and began its march south a short time later and was at the Yuchi (or Euchee) Old Fields by March 2. This place had become an "old fields" due to the defeat of the Yuchi and Fowltown warriors there by McIntosh's command during the Creek War. He now reported from the abandoned Yuchi lands that his movement was progressing slowly due to high water in the creeks and swamps. He noted the capture of three enemy warriors, reporting that he had them "in strings, carrying them to Fort Gains." All three had been involved in the Scott Massacre and one had been wounded in that action.[1]

Major Enos Cutler, commanding at Fort Gaines, reported two days later that the Creeks had reached Eufaula town on the west side of the river near the present city of the same name:

> McIntosh is at Ufala with about seven hundred Indians, and out of provisions. I have written to him that he must bring meat with him. A citizen arrived last night from Fort Mitchell, who tells me the Hogs left there on the 2nd Inst. and that the boat will be ready to move this day. He says it will bring provisions unless the Tennessee troops eat it. I have sent a third express for salt to Colo. Brearly but have not yet heard from him.
>
> I have collected the cattle that can be driven on the other side of the river, twenty five in number, and almost all small and poor.[2]

The force under Gen. McIntosh was actually closer to 900 strong. The other 600 men of the Creek Brigade were scouring the area between the

Chattahoochee and Flint Rivers under the command of Majors Noble Kennard and George Lovett. That command would join the main army under Gen. Jackson on March 6, 1818.

Major Cutler found himself in a bit of a pinch at Fort Gaines as McIntosh approached with his 900 hungry warriors. The major had been ordered to send all available provisions to Fort Scott, but the Creeks were expected to arrive at any minute and would expect to be fed. Lt. Col. Arbuckle at Fort Scott increased the pressure on his subordinate by telling him on March 5 that he must in no uncertain terms send food without delay:

> Captn. Burch arrived here on the night of the 3rd inst. with less than half the quantity of corn I had expected to receive. You must have a boat fitted up without delay and send more, apprising me of the time of Departure from Fort Gaines, and you will have secured for this post at least five hundred Bushels of corn let the calls be what they may from other quarters. Some salt must be sent here without a moment's delay if you can obtain it from any quarter.
>
> What has become of Col. Brearley and his supply from Fort Mitchell? For or five days will leave us without bread, when the corn will be our last resort. Many are the disappointments we have met with, and I now have no hopes of supplies from the Agency. Should supplies be in the Bay as may be released from that quarter in seventeen days, with the present prospects the Tennessee horse ought to make for Georgia, tell them go. Our meat will be out nearly as soon as our bread, therefore you must provide it for us if possible. Let me hear from you immediately.[3]

The situation on the frontier was made even more difficult at this time when news arrived that the boat carrying Gen. Gaines and emergency supplies down the Flint River to Fort Scott had struck a rock and sank. Several men were dead and the general was missing. Scouting, including one led by the chief Onis Hadjo, were sent out from Fort Gaines and Fort

Scott to search for him but Arbuckle informed Maj. Cutler that the general still had not been found.[4]

Gaines would soon make it safely to Jackson's advancing army. He was hungry, cold and wearing only his pantaloons, but otherwise was unharmed. Gen. McIntosh, meanwhile, arrived at Fort Gaines with his 900 warriors and the three Red Stick prisoners that had participated in the Scott Massacre:

> I wrote you the other day and told you that I had taken 3 prisoners – I carried them to Fort Gaines to the commanding officer, and he told me he would have nothing to do with them, and said to me, you may deal with them by your own laws. We had proof that they were at the destroying of the boat below the fork of Flint river, and one of them was wounded at that time – they were doing mischief to our friend and I knew what was the law between us and the United States; I did not want them to stand on our land, and I have taken their lives.[5]

The execution of the three Red Stick prisoners was the first U.S. retaliation for the attack on Scott's party. The surviving documentation is silent as to the method used in the killings, but shooting or braining with a hatchet or war club was a standard of the times. A fourth prisoner was surrendered to McIntosh by the commanding officer of Fort Gaines and proved to be a son of the Tame King. Since there was no evidence that he had fought against the United States, the general set him free.[6]

The Creeks remained at Fort Gaines for several days, resting and preparing for the next phase of their arduous campaign. When they marched again on March 7, 1818, a steady stream of Red Sticks came in to surrender:

> ...[O]n the Sunday in the evening there was about fourteen of our old enemies came and gave themselves up to us, with their women and children; I sent their women back with some of our own people to the Ufaula and we have taken

> two of the men along with us as pilots. They told me that the Red Ground Chief had got a great many of our enemies collected together to fight and these two men are piloting us to him. About 1 hour after we took these people, ten more came into our camp with white flags and joined us; I sent this to you – I am going to-day, and to-morrow about 9 o'clock the fight will be ended with us – if I conquer the Red Ground Chief, I don't expect to meet as many more in number hereafter – you will hear from me as quick as the fight is over with us.[7]

The Creeks continued down the Chattahoochee River but found Ekanachatte abandoned. They burned the large town then headed west to the Chipola River where they defeated Econchattimico ("Red Ground King") on March 13, 1818, capturing 53 men and 180 women and children. Ten other men were killed when they tried to escape and touched off a firefight remembered today as the Battle of the Upper Chipola.[8]

Francis William Brady, the Quartermaster at Fort Gaines, sent a report to Lt. Col. Arbuckle on the day after McIntosh's departure in which he provided a progress update on a large boat he was building on the riverbank below the fort:

> I shall be able to have my boat completed with her cargo in on the evening of the 12th and shall positively have this at 1 o'clock on the morning of the 13th. I shall construct this Boat in such a way as to carry three hundred bushels if posable. After I have this I shall use every exertion to get to the mouth of the river before sunset, then should I not, I will continue in the night until I get down, therefore I wish you to instruct the officer who may have charge of the Boat that will meet me to go as low down as passable in order that I may see them on my aproach.[9]

Brady also reported that Red Sticks had set off an alarm in the nearby village of Onis Hadjo by telling the women and children there that they would be "carried off." He sent the Indian countryman William Hardridge to restore order before the inhabitants could take to the woods.

The military significance of Fort Gaines diminished considerably over coming weeks, as did the size of its garrison. Maj. Gen. Andrew Jackson reached Fort Scott on March 9, 1818, and crossed the Flint River just 24-hours later to begin his campaign against the Red Sticks and Seminoles. His march into Florida resulted in the destruction of the major Seminole towns of Tallahassee Talofa, Miccosukee and the Suwannee River towns of Boleck and Nero. The latter chief was a maroon who had previously served under Nicolls at Prospect Bluff. Jackson also built Fort Gadsden at the site of the old Negro Fort before capturing the Spanish fort of San Marcos de Apalache (St. Marks) and the capital city of Pensacola.

The significance of Fort Gaines diminished greatly as this campaign went forward. Supplies flowed through the post on their way down to Fort Scott but the size of its garrison was greatly reduced. The fort did play a role during the months after Jackson's march as a stopping point for Red Stick families being sent up the Apalachicola and Chattahoochee Rivers to new homes in the Creek Nation. The stockade provided them a place to rest for a few days and obtain provisions before they continued their journey.

Among those who passed through after the war was Milly Francis, the famed Creek Pocahontas. A daughter of the Prophet Josiah Francis, she had saved the life of an American soldier named Duncan McKrimmon. Army officers and civilians alike were fascinated by her and treated her kindly as she made the long journey back to the nation with her mother and sister. The Prophet himself was executed by Jackson's order after he was captured at San Marcos de Apalache.

---

[1] Brig. Gen. William McIntosh to Maj. Daniel Hughes, March 2, 1818, Camden Gazette, April 11, 1818, p. 3.

[2] Maj. E. Cutler to Lt. Col. Matthew Arbuckle, March 4, 1818, Adjutant General, Letters Received, NARA.

[3] Lt. Col. Matthew Arbuckle to Major E. Cutler, March 5, 1818, Andrew Jackson Papers, Library of Congress.

[4] *Ibid.*

[5] William McIntosh to Maj. Daniel Hughes, March 6, 1818.

[6] *Ibid.*

[7] Brig. Gen. William McIntosh to Maj. Daniel Hughes, March 10, 1818, *Camden Gazette*, April 11, 1818, p. 3.

[8] Brig. Gen. William McIntosh to Maj. Daniel Hughes, March 16, 1818, *Camden Gazette*, April 11, 1818, p. 3.

[9] Francis William Brady, Quartermaster of the 4th Infantry, to Lt. Col. Matthew Arbuckle, March 8, 1818, Andrew Jackson Papers, Library of Congress.

CHAPTER NINE

The Remarkable Story of Elizabeth Dill

No history of Fort Gaines would be complete without including the story of Elizabeth Dill. This remarkable woman was taken alive when Red Stick Creeks, Seminoles and maroons attacked a boat commanded by Lt. Richard W. Scott just below the confluence of the Chattahoochee and Flint Rivers on November 30, 1817. She later became a prominent resident of Fort Gaines and lived out her long life within walking distance of the old fort on the bluff.

The following is excerpted from *The Scott Massacre of 1817* by this author:

The bloodiest day of the First Seminole War dawned not much different than other recent days on Florida's Apalachicola River. The Timbora volcano still exerted its influence on the weather of the world and temperatures along the border of Spanish Florida already were falling to levels much lower than normal.

Aboard the open vessel commanded by Lieutenant Richard W. Scott of the 7th U.S. Infantry, men, women and children shivered in the early morning mist. Some of the soldiers shivered from the cold, but nearly half of them shook with the fever that had overcome them on their long journey from the Alabama River to the Apalachicola. On shore and hidden in the trees where they could not benefit even from the meager sunlight of the morning, Creek, Seminole, Yuchi (Euchee) and African warriors shivered as well. It takes time for the sun to rise high enough over the bluffs that tower above the east bank of the river for the woods and swamps below to benefit from its warming rays.

Roughly two miles below the original confluence of the Chattahoochee and Flint Rivers, the course of the Apalachicola makes a wide bend. The site of the confluence is now beneath the waters of Lake Seminole about 5,000 feet above the Jim Woodruff Dam. One mile below the dam, however, the river still swings around the same bend as it begins its southward flow to the Gulf of Mexico. A panoramic view of the curve of the river can be seen from the dock at Chattahoochee Landing and in 1817, as a boat rounded the bend from the South, it would have been possible for its passengers to see straight up the channel to the point of land formed by the confluence.

As Lieutenant Scott's boat came around the bend on the morning of November 30, 1817, the men and women aboard it likely gave a sigh of relief as they spotted the confluence just two miles ahead. They had just passed the landing places of the adjoining villages of the friendly chiefs Mulatto King and Yellow Hair. Located on the Jackson County side of the river just north of today's Gulf Power Company plant, these villages had stood on the high ground overlooking the river swamps since at least the days of the American Revolution. Both towns remained friendly to the United States throughout the First Seminole War, but so far as is known not a single person from either village was seen by the people of Scott's party as they passed by the landings.[1]

As the boat entered the widest part of the arc of the bend, it was pushed hard by the full force of the water pouring from the river's two main tributaries. The Apalachicola was beginning its winter rise, a fact that made its current even stronger. The vessel was pushed from the center of the river towards the east bank as the men pulled hard on their oars to maneuver it against the current and around the bend. Their forward progress stalled as the current ran hard against the side of the boat and drove it ever closer to the bank. All that could be seen there were the trees and bushes of the swamp and the focus of the lieutenant and his men was devoted almost entirely to the navigation of the large bend so that they did not run aground in the shallows.[2]

The chill of the morning replaced by the heat of the adrenalin running through their veins, hundreds of warriors waited in the thick trees and brush that lined the east bank at the point where the boat would be forced closest to shore. Stripped for battle and painted in their traditional colors and designs, they took careful aim with their rifles and muskets and waited for the signal to open fire.

The chiefs and warriors who lined the bank that morning came from a variety of towns and even spoke a variety of languages. There were Hitchiti speakers from Miccosukee, Fowltown and Attapulgas; Muskogee speakers from the Red Stick bands of Homathlemico, Autossee Mico and others; and even the Yuchi-speaking followers of Yuchi Billy, who had come down from their new village in the Old Fields on the high ground to the west of the confluence where the West Bank Overlook stands today. Then there were the African warriors or Black Seminoles. Some of these men spoke English, some spoke Spanish, a few from the Mobile area spoke French and others had arrived so recently from Africa that they still spoke the tongues and dialects of their native continent.[3]

The overall command of the Indian force was attributed at the time to Homathlemico. A Red Stick chief from Alabama, he had fled his home region following Andrew Jackson's victory at Horseshoe Bend. Escaping south into Spanish Florida along with Peter McQueen, Josiah Francis and others, he had managed to keep most of his warriors together and had allied himself with Lieutenant Colonel Nicolls and the British during the remaining months of the War of 1812. The chief has often been confused for the Autossee Mico, another Red Stick leader, but they were separate individuals.[4]

While Homathlemico probably did lead the attack, the force that assembled to attack Lieutenant Scott's boat did not operate with the same degree of command and control seen in a regiment or brigade of the U.S. Army. The warriors from each town or band fought grouped together and under the leadership of their own war chief. The warriors of each of these groups understood the strategy and tactics by which the battle was to be fought, but they functioned more as independent war parties fighting together to achieve a common objective than they did as individual parts of a cohesive organization. On November 30, 1817, however, the organization of the Indian force did not matter as much as its size. Lieutenant Scott had only 20 able-bodied men, while the total strength of Homathlemico's command cannot even be accurately estimated. He must have had at least 500 warriors at his disposal, probably many more. This gave the attackers a numerical superiority of more than 25 to 1 over Scott's command. The difference in firepower was devastating.

Lieutenant Scott and his men were focused almost entirely on getting their boat around the bend and into the straight channel that would take them up to the confluence when the east bank of the Apalachicola River suddenly erupted with a solid wall of flame:

> [The survivors] report that the strength of the current, at the point of the attack, had obliged the lieutenant to keep his boat near the shore; that the Indians had formed along the bank of the river, and were not discovered until their fire commenced; in the first volley of which Lieutenant Scott and his most valuable men fell.[5]

The explosion of gunfire from the trees and bushes along the bank all but annihilated the able-bodied portion of Scott's command. The lieutenant and most of his armed men went down without ever firing a shot. The boat now floated on the current and in minutes was pushed aground in the shallows. The various war cries of the Red Stick Creek, Seminole, Yuchi and African warriors rose above the scene, drowning out the terrified screams of the women and children of Lieutenant Scott's party.

Among the soldiers on the boat that day was a man identified only by his last name, Gray. Badly wounded in the first volley, he was still at Fort Scott when Major General Andrew Jackson arrived there in March 1818 at the head of a brigade of Georgia militiamen. In the campfires of the army camps, Gray described the speed and ferocity with which the attack took place:

> ...As those on board were hooking and jamming (as the boatmen called it) near the bank, and opposite a thick canebrake, the Indians fired on them, killing and wounding most of those on board at the first fire. Those not disabled from the first fire of the Indians made the best fight they could, but all on board were killed except Mrs. Stuart and two soldiers Gray, and another man whose name I have forgot, if I ever knew it; they were both shot, but made their escape by swimming to the opposite shore.[6]

Gray's account of the battle was preserved by Major Thomas Woodward, a noted frontiersman and Georgia militia officer who served with William McIntosh's Creek Brigade during Jackson's Florida campaign. While his memories of the soldier's story were not perfect when he wrote them down forty years later in a letter to John Banks, a Georgia militia soldier who also served in the invasion, Woodward's account remains the only known detailed description of the battle as originally provided by a participant.

Either six or seven soldiers actually survived the battle, not just the two remembered by Woodward, but otherwise the details of his account are consistent with the reports of the fight sent by General Gaines to the Secretary of War, General Jackson and Governor Rabun of Georgia. The "Mrs. Stuart" mentioned by Woodward was Mrs. Elizabeth Stewart, the wife of a soldier from the First Brigade. Her husband was not part of Scott's party, having taken part in the land march to Fort Scott. His wife and six other women (also wives of soldiers) were on board the vessel, along with four small children. Of these eleven civilians, only Mrs. Stewart survived:

> ...Lieut. Scott and his Party...were fired on by a party of Indians about two miles from the mouth of the river, and without being able to make any defence fell into their

> hands, except seven, six of whom came in the succeeding day (five of them wounded). The seventh I understand is at this time with some friendly Indians. The women and children were all killed at that time or since murdered except one who not being wounded is at this time a prisoner with them.[7]

According to Woodward's memories of Gray's account, the warriors waded into the water and stormed the boat as it ran aground in the shallows on the east side of the river. Because Lieutenant Scott and most of his able-bodied men had gone down in the first volley, there was little the sick soldiers, women and children on the vessel could do to defend themselves. In fact, Gray related that the only real resistance put up by the men of Scott's command came in the form of a remarkable last stand by Sergeant Frederick McIntosh from Twiggs' Company, 7th U.S. Infantry:

> *...When he found all on the boat were lost, and nothing more could be done, he went into a little kind of cabin that the Lieutenant had occupied as his quarters, in which was a swivel or small cannon; loaded it, took it on deck, and resting the swivel on one arm ranged it as well as he could, and (the Indians by this time were boarding the boat) with a fire-brand, he set off the swivel, which cleared the boat for a few minutes of Indians. At the firing of the swivel he was thrown overboard and drowned, and this clearing of the Indians from the boat for a short time gave Gray a chance to escape.*[8]

According to Woodward, Sergeant McIntosh was a well-known figure on the Florida frontier. A member of the force that invaded Florida in support of the Patriot Revolt of 1812, McIntosh was described by Woodward as a Scotchman who had served in Colonel Thomas A. Smith's unsuccessful investment of St. Augustine in 1812. Popular with both officers and the enlisted men, McIntosh was said to be a cousin of William

McIntosh, the Coweta chief who served under Jackson in both the Creek War of 1813-1814 and the First Seminole War. Woodward remembered that, "Sergeant McIntosh was a man of giant size, and perhaps more bodily strength than any man I have known in our service."[9]

Woodward, as should be expected, was both accurate and inaccurate in his memories of Sergeant McIntosh as recorded 40 years after the man's death. According to his actual enlistment records, McIntosh was enlisted in the U.S. Rifles by Colonel Thomas Smith between February and April of 1813 for the duration of the War of 1812. Woodward was correct in his memory that McIntosh had been born in Scotland and that he had served in support of the Patriot Revolt in East Florida. His enlistment record confirms that he was from Scotland and that he had enlisted at Camp New Hope in East Florida.[10]

On the other hand, the sergeant was not a large and powerful man as remembered long after the fact by Thomas Woodward. His enlistment record indicates that he was 5'10" tall with blue eyes, fair hair and fair complexion when he enlisted at the age of 27 in 1813. Discharged at the end of the War of 1812, the sergeant left the service for a time but then reenlisted on March 5, 1817, in Twiggs' Company, 7th Infantry, as a sergeant. He came back into the army as a substitute for a soldier with the curious name of Young Blood.[11]

The sergeant's act of heroism in taking up the small cannon in his bare hands and firing it at the warriors as they swarmed over the bulkheads of the boat cost him his life, but created an opportunity for Gray and the other five male survivors to escape. The soldiers able to do so, all but one of whom were wounded, went over the sides of the vessel and swam away under the water. They swam across the current of the Apalachicola and pulled themselves from the river on the Jackson County shore. Others might also have attempted to escape in this way, but if they were severely wounded, the river could have certainly claimed their lives before they reached the opposite bank.

The survivors appear to have been rescued by the inhabitants of the villages of Mulatto King and Yellow Hair on the Jackson County side of the river. As was noted earlier, the chiefs and most of the people of these towns tried to remain at peace with the United States during the war. In notifying Major Muhlenburg of the disastrous fate of Lieutenant Scott's command on December 2, 1817, Major Clinton Wright noted that one of the surviving men was then "with some friendly Indians."[12]

Things did not go well for the wounded men, women and children trapped on the boat. The fate of the most helpless of these was particularly gruesome. Peter Cook, the store clerk of Alexander Arbuthnot, heard accounts of the attack first hand from some of the Seminole or Red Stick participants who described how the children aboard Scott's vessel were put to death. He repeated these descriptions in a letter sent from the Suwannee River to Miss Elizabeth Carney in the Bahamas just six weeks after the Scott Massacre:

> There was a boat that was taken by the Indians, that had in it thirty men, seven women, four small children. There were six of the men got clear, and one woman saved, and all the rest of them got killed. The children were took by the leg, and their brains dashed out against the boat.[13]

The fate of the men and women found wounded in the boat was no better. Killed with hatchets and clubs, they were scalped and their bodies otherwise mutilated. Scalps recognized by the hair as having belonged to the men, women and children of Scott's party were later found adorning a wooden pole in the primary Seminole villages near Lake Miccosukee.

Of the women, later reports indicate that at least two survived the initial bloodshed. One of these was Elizabeth Stewart:

> ...Mrs. Stuart was taken almost lifeless as well as senseless, and was a captive until the day I carried her to your camp. After taking her from the boat, they (the Indians) differed among themselves as to whose slave or

> servant she should be. An Indian by the name of Yellow Hair said he had many years before been sick at or near St. Mary's, and that he felt it a duty to take the woman and treat her kindly, as he was treated so by a white woman when he was among the whites. The matter was left to an old Indian by the name of Bear Head, who decided in favor of Yellow Hair.[14]

The identity of the other woman carried away from the scene of the attack was not recorded and little is known of what happened to her other than that she became too exhausted to keep up with the warriors as they withdrew from the river. She was killed.

The veracity of Woodward's account of the captivity of Mrs. Stewart is difficult to assess. The Yellow Hair mentioned by him could not have been the chief of Yellow Hair's town near the massacre scene or she would have been taken back to Fort Scott. The statement that the Yellow Hair responsible for saving the woman did so to repay a kindness paid to him many years before by a woman on the St. Mary's indicates at least circumstantially that he was a Seminole. It is known for a fact, however, that she was with Peter McQueen's band of Red Sticks when she was freed by Andrew Jackson's army following the Battle of Econfina during the spring of 1818.

The exact number of people killed and wounded in the attack on Scott's party is difficult to determine with precision. The military reports and private letters from officers at Fort Scott dating from the days and weeks after the attacks give various estimates. General Gaines himself reported that Scott's vessel was carrying the lieutenant, 40 soldiers and seven women. Of this number, he reported, six men and one woman survived. The general's estimate, then, would place total losses in the attack at 34 or 35 men and six women killed, four men wounded and one woman – Mrs. Stewart – captured.[15]

This tally was generally supported by a statement that Lieutenant Colonel Matthew Arbuckle added to the November 1817 monthly report for the 7th U.S. Infantry:

> ...Since making out the enclosed report I have recd. The unpleasant news of Lieut. Scott and thirty three or four men, being killed by the Indians on the 30th ultimo; this took place on the Appalachicola River (as the party was ascending in a boat) a short distance below the junction of the Flint and Chattahochie Rivers.[16]

Peter Cook, writing from information provided to him by Indian warriors involved in the attack, estimated the U.S. loss at 24 men, 6 women and 4 children killed. His account agrees with that of General Gaines in its statement that only seven people – six men and one woman – survived the battle. Cook's account provided the lowest number of fatal casualties of the known accounts from the two months after the battle.[17]

The highest estimate appeared in the Savannah *Republican* on December 17, 1817. That account reported that Scott, 44 of his men, 10 women and three children were killed, numbers that combined for a total loss of 58 men, women and children. The paper did not provide information on the source of its data.[18]

A name by name analysis of the enlistment records of the U.S. Army has produced a list of 32 soldiers, including Lieutenant Scott, killed in action, plus one additional man listed as missing and presumed dead. Adding to this number the women and children reported killed and the soldiers reported wounded, a final casualty list can be assembled of 32 men, 6 women and four children killed, 5 men wounded, one woman captured and one man reported missing but presumed dead. One man escaped the attack unharmed. If these numbers are totally inclusive, then the total loss for Scott's party was 42 killed, five wounded, one missing in action and one captured, or a combined total of 49 known killed, wounded, missing and captured.[19]

Other soldiers may also have been killed in the action and the reports of General Gaines and Lieutenant Colonel Arbuckle certainly add support to such a possibility. Both officers placed the total loss in the attack on Scott's party at around 33 or 34 men killed. At the time they wrote their reports, however, they had not been able to communicate with Major Muhlenburg to know how many men from Scott's original detachment had been left behind with that officer on the lower Apalachicola. If the wooden boat assigned to Lieutenant Scott was designed to carry around 40 men, and this is a point worth considering, then Muhlenburg would not have sent it back up to Fort Scott with more people aboard than the vessel was designed to carry.

When the boat left the fort, it was carrying 40 men and no cargo. When the major ordered it back up to the Flint River, he had the clothing stores of the 4th U.S. Infantry placed aboard. When they wrote their reports, Gaines and Arbuckle did not know that part of the vessel's capacity was being used for that purpose. If the boat was designed to carry 40 soldiers, then with part of its burden being used to carry cargo, the smaller estimates of total losses seem more realistic. Peter Cook cited warriors who participated in the attack in placing the total number of people on board Lieutenant Scott's vessel as 30 men, 7 women and 4 children. His number, however, is far below the one that results from a study of the post returns, enlistment records and official reports (i.e. 39 men, 7 women and 4 children).[20]

Without additional information on the size of the vessel, the only conclusion that can be made is that the total U.S. loss in killed, wounded and captured was nearly fifty. The total verifiable loss was 49 with a minimum of 42 men, women and children being killed. The U.S. Army would not experience a day more bloody until Major Francis Dade's party was destroyed eighteen years later at the beginning of the Second Seminole War. It is worth noting that Dade was a 1st lieutenant in the 4th U.S. Infantry when the attack on Scott's party took place. He was absent on recruiting duty and was not at Fort Scott when news of the disaster was received.[21]

For the entire night of November 30, 1817, no one at Fort Scott knew what had happened to Lieutenant Scott and his unfortunate command.

General Gaines undoubtedly hoped that the reinforcements sent down under Captain Clinch were more than sufficient to help the lieutenant complete his passage up to the fort, but on the next day such hopes were replaced by shock:

> Yesterday five of his men came in all wounded. They state, that Lieut. Scott was attacked by the Indians just below the forks of the river, and the whole party killed except themselves. This is truly lamentable. I expect we shall have some very warm work before many days. The whole Indian force is supposed to be 2,800.[22]

The final number of survivors that reached Fort Scott is unclear. In his report to the Secretary of War dated December 2, 1817, the general indicated that six men had come in, four of whom were wounded. On the same day, however, Major Clinton Wright, the assistant adjutant general assigned to General Gaines, penned a warning to Major Muhlenburg, informing him that six men had come in, five of whom were wounded, while a seventh was with friendly Indians. Whether this seventh individual ever reached the fort is not clear.[23]

The names of only two of the wounded have been identified. The first of these was Private William James from Twiggs' Company, 7th U.S. Infantry. Formerly a corporal who had been reduced in rank, he was reported to have been "wounded in action near Fort Apalachicola." This apparently was the name given by U.S. forces to the outpost built one mile below the confluence of the Chattahoochee and Flint Rivers by British troops during the War of 1812. Constructed in 1814, the fort was evacuated the following spring and so far as is known never was occupied again. [24]

The second known survivor of the massacre was the soldier identified only by his last name of Gray. He was mentioned in the account of Thomas Woodward, who reported that Gray was present with Jackson's army during the 1818 Florida Campaign.

It was also known at Fort Scott by the morning of December 2nd that Elizabeth Stewart had survived the attack. In his dispatch to Major

Muhlenburg, Major Wright reported, "The women and children were all killed at that time or since murdered except one who not being wounded is at this time a prisoner with them." Information on her location and condition would arrive steadily at the fort over the next several months, providing tantalizing bits of intelligence to the officers there and to her desperate husband, who was among the men stationed at the post. Contrary to some accounts, he was not one of the men killed in the attack.[25]

Note: Elizabeth Stewart remained in the hands of Peter McQueen's band of Red Sticks through the winter of 1817-1818. As Andrew Jackson invaded Florida in March 1818 and was advancing on the town of Tallahassee Talofa (where the city of Tallahassee stands today), intelligence began to trickle in that the band holding her was not far ahead.

The aftermath of the attack on Lieutenant Scott's party now began to take on even more serious international implications. Additional supplies reached Fort Gadsden on March 24th and the army broke camp the next morning and began its march for Tallahassee and Miccosukee. The route of the march took Jackson back to the north and then eastward around the morass of the Tate's Hell Swamp. He re-entered present-day Gadsden County and reached the Ochlocknee River on the 29th at a point opposite the Leon County bluff that today bears his name.

The river was running high, but the aggressive general ordered his men to begin building canoes and on March 30, 1818, the 2,000 man army crossed the Ochlockonee and on the next day reached the town of Tallahassee Talofa:

> ...On Tuesday, the 31st, arrived at a town called Tallahassee. The Indians had abandoned it before we got there. We passed an old Indian lying near a pond, dead. She had not been dead long from her appearance; she had been left there to die by the Indians who fled before us; she was lying on the ground by some ashes and a dirt pot. We burnt

> the town (this is the present capital of Florida). We found some cattle that day which were distributed amongst the soldiers.[26]

The arrival of the main army at Tallahassee had been preceded by the rapid push forward of a force under Major Twiggs. Intelligence had been received that the band of Red Sticks holding Elizabeth Stewart was at the village and General Jackson attempted to attack them before they could escape with their captive:

> ...We knew long before we re-captured her what band she was with, and had tried to come up with them before...The most tiresome march I ever made was one night in company with the present Gen. Twiggs. He with some soldiers, and I with a party of Indians, trying to rescue her at old Tallahassee, but the Indians had left before we reached the place.[27]

Note: Having failed to recapture Mrs. Stewart, Jackson continued on to the Battle of Miccosukee and then turned south to San Marcos de Apalache at what is now St. Marks, Florida. There he captured the Spanish fort and with it Homathlemico, one of the leaders of the Scott Massacre. The old Red Stick was executed without trial or ceremony. Jackson's next move was a march to the Suwannee River. As he approached the Econfina River, however, the sound of animals could be heard indicating that a large band of Red Sticks was nearby:

The Natural Bridge of the Econfina River is a beautiful and pristine place. Some might call it remote, but it is only a 20 minute drive from Perry, Florida. Tallahassee, meanwhile, is only 45 minutes away, off to the northwest. U.S. Highway 98 passes just a short distance north of the unique natural feature.

Only a real "natural bridge" during dry weather, the Natural Bridge of the Econfina is a place where part of the river's current flows underground for a short distance before rising back to the surface. At normal water levels, the river flows over the natural bridge as well as beneath it and the old crossing place is recognizable only as a shallow place and small waterfall. At high water, even the waterfall disappears beneath the smooth and powerful flow of the Econfina.

Now preserved at the Suwannee River Water Management District's Natural Well Branch tract, the natural bridge was used as a crossing place for hundreds of years. So many people, horses and wagons crossed the river there over the years that the trace of the old road was actually worn down into the rock of the bridge. The trail used by Jackson's army to cross the Econfina in 1818 is still quite visible today. Somewhere in this vicinity is also the battlefield where Elizabeth Stewart was freed from her captors.

Having escaped Jackson's advance on Miccosukee and his subsequent capture of Fort St. Marks, Peter McQueen led his large band of Red Sticks eastward in a slow move for the Suwannee River. He apparently planned to join his warriors with the men of Boleck's band and the several hundred Black Seminole warriors who lived nearby. Together they would have sufficient strength to wage a rearguard action as the women, children, supplies and livestock were evacuated to safety. It was a desperate but slow movement, with the chief and his warriors encumbered by their families, possession, cattle and everything else they owned.

Among the women guarded by McQueen's warriors was the only female survivor of the Scott Massacre, Elizabeth Stewart. How she came to be there is not clear. Some of the chief's men could have participated in the attack on Scott's command, or McQueen could have welcomed followers of Homathlemico into his band after their chief was captured at St. Marks. Also with the women of the slow moving band was a sister of Peter McQueen. She had once been married to an English trader named Powell and her son, a young boy rapidly becoming a man ahead of his time, was then known by the name Billy Powell. He was around nine years old in the spring of 1818, but in later years grew to become the famed Seminole warrior, Osceola.

McQueen's town had been somewhere near that of the Prophet Francis on the Wakulla River and he had been fortunate that he was not with the latter individual when Lieutenant McKeever sailed the *Thomas Shields* into the St. Marks River. Instead, learning of the attack on Miccosukee and almost simultaneous capture of the Creek prophet, McQueen began a desperate effort to get his people to safety.

The rivers and creeks were running high and the movement was painfully slow. The halt of Jackson's army at Fort St. Marks likely gave the chief hope that his effort would succeed. The forces of the American general, however, were converging on him faster than the old Red Stick could move his followers out of harm's way.

Having occupied Fort St. Marks with a strong garrison, Jackson ordered his men to prepare to march and as the soldiers headed out across the marshes that surrounded the fort on the morning of April 9, 1818, they numbered over 2,000 muskets. To the men watching from the ramparts, the army must have presented an impressive sight, its long columns of blue and brown crossing the open marsh and disappearing into the trees.

Jackson followed the old trail that led from St. Marks west to the Suwannee. It looped in a curving path to the northeast around the worst of the coastal lowlands before crossing the Natural Bridge of the Econfina and passing on via a more direct route to the crossing on the Suwannee River near Boleck's town. There were no settlements along the way and the march was through one continuous wilderness.[28]

Apparently alerted as to the general's plan, other commands still moving to reinforce him angled their marches to form junctions with the army along its line of march. On April 10th two full regiments of mounted Tennessee volunteers made contact with Jackson and joined his column. A few regulars also arrived and then, later in the day, Brigadier General McIntosh finally reached the army with his brigade of 1,100 Creek warriors. They had been left behind at Miccosukee to scour the countryside for enemy warriors and enemy cattle. With the arrival of these two forces, the size of the army doubled in a single day. General Jackson now had a force more than capable of sweeping aside any resistance that could be offered by the remaining warriors of the Red Stick and Seminole alliance.[29]

The soldiers and officers of the army had known for some time that the Indian party holding Mrs. Stewart was just ahead of them. The general had ordered Major Twiggs to move against Tallahassee Talofa ahead of the main army after hearing that the unfortunate woman was being held there, but the Seminoles were able to evacuate the town before the major's force arrived. Somewhere in the vicinity of St. Marks the troops again picked up information on Stewart's presence among the Indians known to be withdrawing towards the Suwannee. Jackson knew he was closing in on McQueen, but no one in the army knew the exact whereabouts of the Red Stick chief until the morning of April 12, 1818:

> ...On the morning of the 12th, the officer of the day reported that the sentinels had heard the lowing of cattle and barking of dogs during the night; from which the general was indused to send a runner to General McIntosh, who was encamped a short distance in rear of the army, with instructions to have the country below examined. In the meantime, the army moved slowly in advance.[30]

As Jackson's main force pushed forward and across the Natural Bridge of the Econfina, McIntosh moved his command into the woods south of the trail and began a search for the source of the sounds heard during the night. Major Noble Kenard (or Kinnard) was ordered to advance deeper into the woods and find the location of what was believed to be the Red Stick camp. In short order Kinnard sent back a runner with word that he had discovered a large enemy force and needed immediate reinforcement:

> ...McIntosh moved against them with his whole force. A small detachment of different companies of Tennessee volunteers, under Colonels Dyer and Williamson, (they having joined the army on the evening of the 10th,) were left

> at our encampment to search for horses, and, on hearing the report of Major Kanard, formed themselves into a company under Captain Bell, who was with them, and moved to attack the enemy, whom they found near a large swamp endeavoring to move off.[31]

The pursuit of Peter McQueen finally came to an end. When McIntosh attacked, the chief was trying to get the women and children and large cattle herd to safety. As the Creek warriors and Tennessee volunteers appeared in the woods behind him, McQueen ordered his warriors into action. The size of the force at his command was no match for McIntosh's brigade, but most of his warriors had fought in some of the bitterest actions of the Creek War of 1813-1814. The chief and his men were seasoned and determined fighters:

> ...McIntosh with a part of his warriors, attacked a party of hostile Indians. The engagement continued about two hours with much spirit, when the hostiles retreated, leaving their women, children and property of all kinds to the mercy of the conquerors – Sustaining a loss of 37 killed on the field, and two wounded, and a number of prisoners. The number of Indians engaged was differently represented by different prisoners. McIntosh had three men killed, and several wounded.[32]

In the midst of the battle, as war cries, gunfire and smoke filled the swamp along the margin of the Econfina River, a woman could be heard calling for help. Elizabeth Stewart had been found:

> ...Shortly after the firing commenced, we could hear a female voice in the English language calling for help, but she was concealed from our view. The hostile Indians, though greatly inferior in number to our whole force, had the advantage of the ground, it being a dense thicket, and

> kept the party that first attacked at bay until Gen. McIntosh arrived with the main force. McIntosh, though raised among savages, was a General; yes, he was one of God's make of Generals. I could hear his voice above the din of firearms — "Save the white woman! Save the Indian women and children."[33]

Mrs. Stewart had taken advantage of the confusion created by the sudden attack to escape from those holding her and find shelter among the thick palmetto that grew on the margin of the swamp. As the battle intensified and McIntosh's main force came up, she began to call for help.

There are some discrepancies about what happened next. Thomas Woodward, who described the Battle of Econfina some 40 years later, claimed that he was directed by General McIntosh in person to go with a few other men and save the woman:

> ...All this time Mrs. Stuart was between the fires of the combatants. McIntosh said to me, "Chulatarla Emathla, you, Brown and Mitchell, go to that woman." (Chulatarle Emathla was the name I was known by among the Indians.) Mitchell was a good soldier and a bad cripple from rheumatism. He dismounted from his horse and said, "Boys, let me lead the way." We made the charge with some Uchees and Creeks, but Mitchell, poor fellow, was soon left behind, in consequence of his inability to travel on foot.[34]

Woodward's account was written in a letter to John Banks, the former Georgia militia private who also left a firsthand account of Jackson's campaign. Both men were present at the time, although Banks was with the main column while Woodward was on the battlefield itself. Woodward probably magnified his own importance along with that of his friends in his version – military records indicate the detachment that saved Mrs. Stewart was led by Major Noble Kinnard – but his account is the only known firsthand description of her rescue:

> ...I can see her now, squatted in the saw palmetto, among a few dwarf cabbage trees, surrounded by a group of Indian women. There I saw Brown kill an Indian, and I got my riflestock shot off just back of the lock. Old Jack Carter came up with my horse shortly after we cut off the woman from the warriors. I got his musket and used it until the fight ended. You saw her (Mrs. Stuart) when she reached the camp, and recollect her appearance better than I can describe it.[35]

As the battle intensified, the heavy firing could be heard by the soldiers of Jackson's main column, which had moved forward about six miles from the scene of the action. McQueen's warriors were outnumbered, but waged the fiercest battle of the 1818 campaign. They also paid heavily in blood:

> ...There seemed to be a considerable number collected there. When we first began to fight them, they were in a bad swamp, and fought us there for about an hour, when they ran, and we followed them three miles. They fought us in all about three hours. We killed 37 of them, and took 98 women and children and six men prisoners, and about 700 head of cattle and a number of horses, with a good many hogs and some corn. We lost three killed and had five wounded.[36]

The nature of the fight and difficulty of the ground made it impossible for McIntosh and his officers to accurately estimate the strength of the Red Stick force. The prisoners they captured indicated to them, however, that numerous towns were represented on the field:

> ...Our prisoners tell us that there was 120 warriors from six different towns. From what we saw I believe there was more than they say, as some of our prisoners say there was

> 200 of them. Tom Woodward and Mr. Brown, and your Son, our Agent, and all the white men that live in our country, were with us through the whole fight, and fought well. All my officers fought so well I do not know which is the bravest. They all fought like men and run their enemies.[37]

The report by General McIntosh was addressed to Indian Agent David B. Mitchell and it was his son, William "Billy" Mitchell, to whom the Creek leader referred in the account. His written "talk", as he described it, also confirmed the presence of Major Woodward in the fight. As he continued his report, the general also made reference to the rescue of Elizabeth Stewart and the presence of her father and spouse with the army at the time of the battle:

> ...There was among the Hostiles a woman that was in the boat where our friends the white people were killed on the river below Fort Scott. We gave her to her friends – her husband and father are with general Jackson – Major Kinnard took her himself.[38]

Note: Elizabeth's rescue at the Battle of Econfina was a topic of great interest and received widespread coverage in newspapers of the time. Delicate sensibilities of the time prevented those who saw her from repeating much of what she told them of her treatment while in the hands of the Red Sticks. Now back with her husband and father, she was carried to Georgia where she would spend the rest of her life.

How and when Elizabeth reached Georgia is not clear. She was returned to her husband and father by Brigadier General William McIntosh's staff following the Battle of Econfina. Whether she remained with Jackson's main army or returned north with the Georgia militia is not known. Her husband was a soldier of the First Brigade but few details have been uncovered about him other than that he died within a few years of her release from captivity at the Battle of Econfina.

John and Mary Lou Missall, in their 2015 novel *Elizabeth's War* speculate that her husband was John Stuart, a sergeant in Company G, 7th Infantry. He was a Kentucky native who enlisted in as a private in the 39th Infantry on July 20, 1814. He was moved to the 7th Infantry when the army was reorganized following the War of 1812. He eventually went on to be commissioned as an officer and served west of the Mississippi at Fort Smith, Fort Gibson and Fort Coffee, dying at the last of these posts on December 8, 1838.[39]

The Missalls may be correct and that this John Stuart was Elizabeth's husband. The obvious implication is that he abandoned her to fend for herself on the Georgia frontier following her return from captivity. This was not a good way to become an officer in the honor-conscious U.S. Army of the early 19th century and no documentation has been found to show that this John Stuart was Elizabeth's husband. All that can be said without further documentation is that he was a sergeant in the 7th Infantry at the time of her captivity. It should also be noted that when she applied for a War of 1812 widow's pension in later years, she did so in the name of her second husband, not this John Stuart.

More solid information is available about Elizabeth's second husband. The marriage records in Early County, Georgia, show that Elizabeth remarried John Dill on September 25, 1821. The present Clay County was then part of Early County and John Dill was a well-known merchant in the town of Fort Gaines, which grew up around the log fort of the same name. The fact that she remarried in Fort Gaines just two years after her release from captivity indicates that if Elizabeth ever left the frontier of Southwest Georgia, it was not for long.[40]

Tradition in Fort Gaines holds that General Dill, as he is remembered there, was an officer on the staff of Major General Edmund P. Gaines and a one-time commander of the post. Actual military records tell a somewhat different story. A native of South Carolina, Dill had served as a private in Captain Turner's Company D, 3rd South Carolina Militia from November 6,

1814 until March 12, 1815. He was sick at the time of his discharge but had served a total of four months and 24 days and was paid $38 for his service.[41]

He appears to have reenlisted in the 39th Infantry by June 1815 and was transferred to Company G, 7th U.S. Infantry during the post-war consolidation of the army. He served as a sergeant but was briefly reduced to the ranks before being promoted to sergeant major on April 1, 1818, the day that Andrew Jackson attacked Miccosukee. He was discharged on September 20, 1819, and soon opened a mercantile business at Fort Gaines where a thriving settlement was growing up around the fort. There is no known documentation to suggest that he was ever the commander of the fort.

By the time the troops headed west for Fort Smith, Arkansas, in September of 1821, Fort Gaines had become a small town and important river port for a thriving agricultural region. What may have been the first house lived in by John and Elizabeth Dill still stands near the edge of the bluff at Fort Gaines. By today's standards it is a simple white wood-frame structure, but by the standards of 1821 it was impressive. It overlooks the site of the original fort as well as the earthwork remains and cannon of a battery constructed by the Confederates during the War Between the States. Called the toll house because it was associated with one of the wooden bridges that spanned the Chattahoochee River at Fort Gaines, the house was once owned by John Dill.

Mr. and Mrs. Dill built a second and much more magnificent home by around 1827. Now known as the "John Dill House," it stands on Washington Street near its intersection of Commerce Street in Fort Gaines. It was here the couple spent the most productive years of their lives.

Legend in Fort Gaines holds that while she was in captivity with the Red Sticks, Mrs. Stewart made a fortune through her own determination and ingenuity. The warriors of the various bands were then predatory raids against homes along the frontier and often came back to the camps in Florida loaded down with plunder. The horses and cows they brought back had obvious value, as did clothing, food and gold or silver coin. The paper money taken in such raids, however, was of no value to the Indians and they often threw it away onto the ground.[42]

Mrs. Dill (then Mrs. Stewart), of course, recognized the value of the paper being tossed away by the raiding parties and began to collect it and secret it away. By the time she was rescued by Major Kinnard at the Battle of Econfina, she had accumulated a small fortune. The money, it is said, helped the couple establish a mercantile empire in Fort Gaines and build two homes there, both of which still can be seen today.[43]

Whether the story is true or not, the Dills did accumulate wealth far above that of most of their neighbors. As their wealth grew, so too did his prominence in the region. By 1830, for example, he had been elected to the rank of major in the local militia regiment and was a key figure in the committee selected to organize that year's 4th of July celebration in Fort Gaines. His fellow committee members elected him as their chairman and he began the festivities with a toast to President Thomas Jefferson, who had died four years earlier. "He was a great and good man," Dill spoke aloud to the group, "his principals, the American political text book."[44]

One of the other toasts that day drew widespread approval when it celebrated the signing of the Indian Removal Act of 1830 by President Andrew Jackson:

> …The Indian Bill; we hail it as a triumph of justice in favor of our slandered and oppressed State, and as a galling proof to those damnable Heralds, and their supporters, the National Journal, New York Daily Advertiser, New York Commercial Advertister, New England Palladium, Harrisburg Intelligencer, and Boston Patriot, with their satellites. Envy, hatred, outrage, devastation, and destruction, fiends like with a daring impudence stalking over the fairest portions of our land, struggling with a death like determination to wither and utterly annihilate the laureled wreath that binds our Federal Union. That Georgia in the majesty of her rights will be heard, the shafts of their calumny fall harmless at her shrine.[45]

The newspapers named in the toast, of course, had opposed the Indian Removal Act, a piece of legislation that drew wide favor in Georgia, Florida and Alabama. It authorized President Jackson to negotiate with Indian nations for their removal to new lands west of the Mississippi. The original intent of the act was for the Creek, Choctaw, Seminole, Cherokee and Chickasaw nations to be given the option of either remaining where they were and living under the laws of the individual states, or of relocating to new lands in what is now Oklahoma where they could retain some self-rule. The actual result, of course, was widespread violence and the forced removal of tens of thousands of people west on what became known as the Trail of Tears.

At the time of the 4th of July celebration in1830, Fort Gaines was just south of and across the Chattahoochee River from what remained of the Creek Nation. The First Seminole War had ended only twelve years before and the animosity that existed between the frontier settlers and the Creeks, particularly the Hitchiti and Yuchi who lived along the Chattahoochee River, was marked and intense. Men like John Dill, whose wife had spent five months in captivity, were fiercely dedicated to the removal of the Creek Indians from their traditional homes to new lands in the west.

A milestone was marked in Elizabeth's life in 1832 when she gave birth to a son, John P. Dill. By that point she was comfortably established in a large and beautiful home and her husband was a prominent and successful businessman and civic leader. The brutality she had seen on November 30, 1817, must have seemed far removed, but it was not long before the memories came surging back.

Major Dill was an ally and associate of William Wellborn, who soon played a key role in enforcing the removal of the Creeks from Alabama and who led troops against them in their last major fight with the whites at the Battle of Hobdy's Bridge in 1837. On January 10, 1834, Wellborn published the Executive Order from Milledgeville that promoted 26 men to the rank of colonel in the Georgia State Militia and designated them to serve as Aides-de-Camp to the state's commander in chief, Governor Wilson Lumpkin. John Dill was among them.[46]

Reappointed to the same role in the administration of Governor William Schley on January 13, 1836, Dill served as a colonel of the second brigade and aide-de-camp to the governor during the Creek War of 1836. Fort Gaines was on the very front of that war and, ironically, a portion of the warriors fighting against the United States was led by Neamathla himself.[47]

It was in his capacity as colonel, Dill joined two other officers in signing a letter to Governor William Schley in which they appealed for help to deal with the inability of the citizens of Fort Gaines to defend themselves against expected Indian attack:

> ...Rumors daily reach us of parties of these Indians, sometimes as high as seventy or [eighty] in company, having murdered in different parts of the country east of the Chatahoochee; and from various indications we have but too much reason to apprehend that the issues recently witnessed in East Florida, will be reenacted here. Our object in writing this letter is to apprise your Excellency that we are almost entirely destitute of arms, for our defence, having to depend exclusively upon such as individuals may happen to possess, and which would be by no means effective in an Indian war.[48]

How Mrs. Dill must have viewed such rumors just nineteen years after she had somehow survived the bloody destruction of Lieutenant Scott's party can be imagined. She must have remembered the scenes enacted before her eyes in 1817, scenes that she certainly hoped would never be enacted again. Such hopes, if she entertained them, were soon dashed. A portion of the Creeks rose against the whites in the spring and summer of 1836. Settlers on their lands were driven off or killed and the Yuchi under Jim Henry crossed the Chattahoochee River and destroyed the town of Roanoke upstream from Fort Gaines in a deadly attack.

The Creek War of 1836 was a desperate last stand by an outnumbered group of Creeks and one that was doomed to fail even before it started. Creek resistance crumbled after the old chief Neamathla was captured. The proud people of the nation were sent west on the Trail of Tears and untold numbers died along the way.

Fortunately for Elizabeth, the war brought no repeat of the captivity she had experienced 20 years before. John Dill served in the Georgia militia for at least another decade and in 1847 he was reported to be the brigadier general of the 1st Brigade. This service was the origin of his title of "general," by which he is often referred today.[49]

General Dill lived until the 1850s and spent the rest of his life as a prominent and successful businessman who owned mercantile establishments, a brickyard and a cotton warehouse. After he passed away, Elizabeth applied for and received a pension based on his War of 1812 service. She collected $3.50 per month for the rest of her life. By 1860, Elizabeth Dill was living in the home of James and Sarah Touson (Towson). Her personal wealth was reported by the census taker to be in the range of $5,000, an impressive sum for a 68-year-old widow who had lived much of her life on the frontier. She died in Fort Gaines on September 5, 1864, and was buried in the town's Old Pioneer Cemetery alongside her husband.[50]

---

[1] Capt. Hugh Young, "A Topographical Memoir of East and West Florida," 1818.
[2] Maj. Gen. Edmund P. Gaines to the Secretary of War, December 2, 1817, *American State Papers*, Indian Affairs, Volume II, p. 687.
[3] List of participating groups assembled from numerous U.S. Army reports, 1817-1818, that identify the village affiliations of members of the attacking force.
[4] Maj. Gen. Andrew Jackson to John C. Calhoun, Secretary of War, (Insert Date and Info)
[5] Maj. Gen. Edmund P. Gaines to the Secretary of War, December 2, 1817, *American State Papers*, Indian Affairs, Volume II, p. 687.
[6] Gen. Thomas S. Woodward to Col. John Banks, June 16, 1858, *Woodward's Reminisences*.
[7] Maj. Clinton Wright, Assistant Adjutant General, to Maj. Peter Muhlenburg, December 2, 1817, Office of the Adjutant General, Letters Received, 1805-1821, National Archives.
[8] Gen. Thomas S. Woodward to Col. John Banks, June 16, 1858.
[9] *Ibid.*
[10] U.S. Army, Register of Enlistments, 1798-1815, National Archives.
[11] *Ibid.*
[12] Maj. Clinton Wright, Assistant Adjutant General, to Maj. Peter Muhlenburg, December 2, 1817.

[13] Peter B. Cook to Elizabeth A. Carney, January 19, 1818, included in Message of the President of the U. States to Congress, 25th March, 1818, published in the *New York Mercantile Advertiser*, January 6, 1819, p.2.
[14] Gen. Thomas S. Woodward to Col. John Banks, June 16, 1858.
[15] Maj. Gen. Edmund P. Gaines to the Secretary of War, December 2, 1817; Maj. Gen. Edmund P. Gaines to Gov. William Rabun, December 2, 1817.
[16] Lt. Col. Matthew Arbuckle to Brig. Gen. D. Parker and Staff, December 7, 1817, enclosed on the Monthly Report of the 7th U.S. Infantry for November 1817, Adjutant General's Office, Letters Received, 1805-1821.
[17] Peter B. Cook to Elizabeth A. Carney, January 19, 1818.
[18] Savannah *Republican* December 17, 1817.
[19] U.S. Army Enlistment Registers, 1798 -
[20] Maj. Gen. Edmund P. Gaines to the Secretary of War, December 2, 1817; Maj. Gen. Edmund P. Gaines to Gov. William Rabun, December 2, 1817; Peter B. Cook to Elizabeth A. Carney, January 19, 1818; U.S. Army Registers of Enlistment, 1798 - ; Lt. Col. Matthew Arbuckle to Brig. Gen. D. Parker and Staff, December 7, 1817.
[21] U.S. Army Register of Enlistments, 1798-1815, entry for Francis L. Dade.
[22] Letter from an officer at Fort Scott to his father in Baltimore, December 2, 1817, published in the *Massachusetts Spy*, December 31, 1817, p. 2.
[23] Maj. Gen. Edmund P. Gaines to the Secretary of War, December 2, 1817; Maj. Clinton Wright to Maj. Peter Muhlenburg, December 2, 1817, Office of the Adjutant General, Letters Received, 1805-1821.
[24] U.S. Army Enlistment Registers.
[25] Maj. Clinton Wright to Maj. Peter Muhlenburg, December 2, 1817.
[26] John Banks, *Diary of John Banks*, 1936, pp. 9-14.
[27] Thomas Woodward to John Banks, June 16, 1858, (add reference)
[28] Capt. Hugh Young, "A Topographical Memoir of East and West Florida with Itineraries," 1818, National Archives.
[29] Report dated Milledgeville, Georgia, May 5, 1818, citing an officer direct from the army, published in the *Weekly Aurora*, May 25, 1818, p. 111.
[30] Maj. Robert Butler, Adjutant General, to Brig. Gen. Daniel Parker, Adjutant & Inspector General, May 3, 1818, *American State Papers*, Military Affairs, Volume 1, p. 703.
[31] *Ibid.*
[32] Report dated Milledgeville, Georgia, May 5, 1818, citing an officer direct from the army, published in the *Weekly Aurora*, May 25, 1818, p. 111.
[33] Gen. Thomas Woodward to Col. John Banks, June 16, 1858, included in (add reference)
[34] *Ibid.*
[35] *Ibid.*
[36] Brig. Gen. William McIntosh to David B. Mitchell, Agent for Indian Affairs, April 13, 1818, *Berks and Schuylkill Journal*, May 16, 1818, p. 2.
[37] *Ibid.*
[38] *Ibid.*
[39] John Missall and Mary Lou Missall, *Elizabeth's War: A Novel of the First Seminole War*, Florida Historical Society Press, Cocoa, FL, 2015, p. 459.
[40] Jordan Dodd, *Georgia Marriages to 1850* [database on-line], Provo, UT, USA: Ancestry.com Operations Inc, 1997.
[41] U.S. Army Register of Enlistments, 1798- ; Service Record of Private John Dill, State Militia Records, South Carolina State Archives.

[42] Traditional story still told in Fort Gaines.
[43] *Ibid.*
[44] "4th of July at Fort Gaines, Geo.," *Georgia Journal*, July 24, 1830, p. 3.
[45] *Ibid.*
[46] Executive Order dated Milledgeville, January 10, 1834, published in the Macon *Weekly Telegraph*, January 23, 1834, p. 3.
[47] Executive Order dated Milledgeville, January 13, 1836, published in the Macon *Weekly Telegraph*, January 28, 1836, p. 3.
[48] J. Patterson, A. McGinty and J. Dill to Gov. William Schley, January 29, 1836.
[49] Eileen Babb McAdams, "Georgia Militia 1847, Major and Brigadier Generals," (List of officers assembled from *Augusta Chronicle*, March 31, 1848), U.S. Genweb.
[50] U.S. Census for District 749, Clay County, Georgia, 1860.

CHAPTER TEN

The Forts on the Bluff

Fort Gaines remained an active military post until 1821, but its role was much reduced. No more than a small detachment was kept there from March 1818 until the post was evacuated in August or early September 1821. The fort continued to stand watch over the southern border of the Creek Nation, but no major problems occurred during its final active years. Its primary importance during the last three years of its existence was as a way station for supplies on their way down to Fort Scott and Fort Gadsden. Soldiers and officers also stopped at the fort to spend the night as they came and went from those posts.

Patrols traveled the road between Fort Gaines and Fort Scott on a regular basis but the fear of a Creek or Seminole attack soon faded. The eternal war between officers and enlisted men, however, continued. One interesting story was written by Charles Martin Gray, a South Carolinian who served in the 7th Infantry from 1819 to 1829. It was then the custom for enlisted men to carry officers over creeks and streams but Gray had a severe dislike for both the custom and the commander of his patrol, Lt. Richard Wash. The soldiers were marching from Fort Scott to Fort Gaines and when they reached Kolomoki Creek in what is now Early County, Wash picked Gray to carry him across:

> I began to reel and stagger under the weight that oppressed me, but recovering proceeded mildly forward until, when making the very middle of the swollen current, I stumbled…and fell in the waters and…disengaged myself entirely from any superincumbent load. The gallant Lieutenant to his great discomfiture, and to the inordinate merriment of all the men and officers present, was thus compelled to struggle alone…while his rich and gaudy uniform was soiled and begrimed with the mud, and rent in shreds by the rocks.[1]

Charles Martin Gray had other memories of his service on the Georgia frontier and they were not as humorous. One was of how Maj. David E. Twiggs punished a musician for leaving camp without permission:

> [He] pulled off his own coat, rolled up his sleeves, and inflicted upon his bare back, with a horse whip, twenty-five lashes, which made the blood spout and trickle down his manly form, and that scarred the skin at every stroke. At another time, for some small offense, he sentenced one of his command to pitch straws against the wind, for four or five hours without intermission. The wind was blowing a gale, and the penalty was that he should receive one lash for every straw he failed to produce. At the end of this delightful exercise…he found himself minus many a straw, and crowned with many a stripe, for he was compelled to pitch the straws as high in the air, as his strength, and the boisterous elements would allow, and an unrelenting Orderly was present to report minutely every failure either of his strength or his skill.[2]

One of the last mentions of the original Fort Gaines from military records appeared in April 1821. A tabulation of occupied U.S. Army posts in Department No. 8 showed that the fort was then held by 15 men under Lt. Branch of the 7th Infantry.[3]

The garrison only got smaller and the men of the 7th Infantry began to prepare for the expected evacuation of their posts on the Florida border. Spain had agreed to transfer her centuries old colony to the United States and there would no longer be a need for troops to guard the national boundary. The last soldiers were ordered to evacuate Fort Gaines in either late August or early September of 1821 and make their way down to Fort Scott. Whether they went by land or water is not known, but travel by boat would have made it easier for them to carry the supplies of the post with them. Fort Scott was evacuated just days later as the 7th Infantry began its long journey to new posts on the Arkansas and Red Rivers west of the Mississippi. It was not a pleasant trip:

> …Having descended the Appalachicola, and being encamped near its mouth, the troops were exposed to violent storms of wind and rain, which caused a great augmentation of the sick list. Transportation having at length arrived, the troops embarked for New Orleans in seven sloops and schooners – he sick being stowed away with the other men and the baggage of their companies respectively; and until their arrival at the bayou St. John they were, by this arrangement in most of the vessels, deprived of medical aid. Here the men suffered exceedingly from the quality of the water, which had been put into casks containing the impure lees of wine. The cases of dysentery were consequently much increased in number, and rendered more fatal."[4]

It was the custom of the military to leave abandoned forts standing and the original Fort Gaines probably remained intact for at least a few years. Settlers usually raided such posts for useful items such as windows, hinges, nails, bricks, wood and shingles. The community that continues to bear the name of the old fort was growing and anything that could be used was probably salvaged quickly. How long the blockhouses or any of the pickets remained standing is not known, but any ruins clearly had far outlived their military usefulness by the time of the Creek War of 1836. Fifteen years had passed since the departure of the last soldiers and the people of Fort Gaines found themselves with no fortification in which to seek shelter in the event of a Native American attack.

The final Creek War erupted in the spring of 1836 when Neamathla, Jim Henry and other chiefs led an alliance of Yuchi and Hitchiti groups, in a rebellion against efforts to force them to abandon the last remaining sliver of their lands. Henry (who later became a Methodist minister in what is now Oklahoma under the name James McHenry) led a devastating raid against the town of Roanoke in Stewart County, Georgia, burning its structures to the ground. The warriors killed most of the handful of men who remained behind to defend the community after its women and children been evacuated to the safety of nearby Lumpkin.

The raid on Roanoke, which stood just up the Chattahoochee from Fort Gaines, prompted great alarm. Citizens requisitioned any heavy timbers they could find and built a new fort for their own defense:

> ...We have built us a temporary Fort here, in doing which, we had to press all the Scantling & plank, Sills, & house framings, for it was built in a hurry, hearing that the Indians was on the way down from Roanoke., about ¼ of this Lumber is spoilt in Sawing, Short, & Cutting port holes, - We expect to be paid for the same, through the state from the Genl. Government.[5]

John Dill appealed to Governor Schley to countermand orders requiring the militia companies from Fort Gaines and Early County to assemble with the main Georgia army at Fort Twiggs near Cusseta. The town, he reported, had become a point of last refuge for the citizens and the troops were needed there to protect them:

> ...[I]f any needs protection it is us. The point of the Creek Nation is only about four miles distant from Fort Gaines – and the white inhabitants of the nation has fled from the nation entire except Irwinton [i.e. Eufaula, Alabama], which is not yet abandoned by the inhabitants and which is daily expected to suffer the same fate of Roanoke, if so, Fort Gaines next, perhaps before, for we are in a defenceless situation at the present.[6]

Dill pointed out to Schley that the fort was "the refuge for the women and children of this section." Included among the civilians he sought to protect, of course, was Elizabeth. The news from Roanoke had electrified the community and near panic ensued as citizens from throughout the area flooded into town with the handful of belongings they could cary.

Dill, now a colonel in the militia, defied orders and detained 18 drafted men from Early County to help protect the makeshift fort. More than 100 women and children had come to the town from Irwinton (Eufaula), Alabama, and the houses and buildings were crowded with suffering civilians. Exceeding his authority, Dill had formed a force to protect these people and prevailed upon the governor to approve of his actions. By raising two additional companies to augment the Fort Gaines Guards, he reported that he enabled the community to "keep a guard out at night which is of great relief to our women."[7]

Fighting did take place north, west and east of Fort Gaines, but the town itself was never attacked by the Creeks. The war ended quickly and most of the Creek men, women and children were forced west on the Trail of Tears. Neamathla, now over 80 years old, went west in irons with no complaint or show of emotion. The second Fort Gaines was probably dismantled in short order and the building materials scavenged for its construction returned to their original purpose.

The historic bluff at Fort Gaines would see one final military incarnation. Confederate engineers tasked with defending the Chattahoochee River valley during the War Between the States or Civil War recognized the importance of the bluff. After surveying both the Apalachicola and Chattahoochee Rivers in the fall of 1862, Capt. Theodore Moreno recommended that obstructions and a battery of heavy artillery be placed at Fort Gaines. A highly-regarded engineer, Moreno was doing his best to defend the river and particularly the industrial city of Columbus with the means at his disposal. His superior, Maj. A.L. Rives at the Engineer Bureau in Richmond, approved of the concept but told Moreno that he could not supply heavier and more modern cannon than the 32-pounders already on the river:

> ...I am sorry to inform you, after due inquiry, that the supply of ordnance is so limited that nothing better can be suggested apparently at present than to have the 18 and 24 pounders at Alum Bluff mounted on siege carriages for defending the lower obstructions at Rock Bluff, while the five 32-pounders are mounted at Fort Gaines to defend the upper in its vicinity.
>
> At both of these points it might be well to make further preparations for the heavier ordnance called for by you, and which perhaps can be furnished at a future day. The necessary implements, carriages, &c., to put the ordnance now on the river in a complete state of efficiency can, I am informed by the ordnance department, be obtained from the arsenal at Macon, Ga., and it would be well for you to suggest to the senior captain of the two artillery companies mentioned in your letter to make the necessary requisition on the officer in charge of the arsenal, subject to the approval of the general commanding the department.[8]

Rives also offered suggestions for obstructing the river but it is unclear how serious Moreno was about doing so since steamboat traffic continued on the Chattahoochee from Columbus down to Florida. He recommended that parallel rows of log cribs be submerged in the river and that floating log rafts then be chained to them. These rafts would move up and down with the level of the river to obstruct it to any gunboats regardless of the season. The cannon on the bluff, of course, would protect the obstructions.[9]

Obstructions were placed at the Narrows of the Apalachicola River, but the Chattahoochee was never blocked at Fort Gaines. Major Rives' recommendation that five 32-pounders be placed on the bluff was also never followed. An array of high ranking officers soon became involved in the project, among them Gen. P.G.T. Beauregard who exercised overall command of the river defenses from his headquarters in Charleston, South Carolina. Through his chief of staff Brig. Gen. Thomas Jordan, he rearranged the proposed placement of the cannons on the river system:

> ...The Chattahoochee is to be obstructed at Fort Gaines, and a battery to be erected to cover the obstructions for two 32 and one 24 pounder pieces. At Rock Bluff, 54 miles above the junction with Flint River, another obstruction is to be established, with three batteries commanding it, one of three 32-pounders, one for two 24-pounders, and the third for two 18-pounder guns. At the Narrows, at Fulton's Bend, on the Apalachicola, 16 miles below junction with the Flint River, other obstructions and a battery for one 24 and one 18 pounder gun, are likewise to be constructed. In this way will be disposed the twelve pieces which Captain Moreno has available at present. The positions just named are all regarded as favorable for the ends in view.[10]

Gen. Beauregard had served on the Apalachicola River during the Second Seminole War (1835-1842) but his memory of locations and landmarks had clearly faded. Rock Bluff, which his chief of staff located 54 miles above the confluence of the Chattahoochee and Flint Rivers, is in fact on the upper Apalachicola River. The Narrows, which Jordan placed 16 miles below the forks, is actually far down the Apalachicola near its confluence with the Chipola River.

The new plan reduced the size of the proposed battery at Fort Gaines from five 32-pounders to two 32-pounders and one 24-pounder. Before the orders could even be sent, however, they were altered in a post script:

> Since the foregoing was written Captain Moreno has been telegraphed to construct the battery at the Narrows for three guns instead of two, and to substitute two 32-pounders from Fort Gaines for the 18-pounder originally designed for the Narrows' work.
>
> Captain Moreno will be further instructed to examine Flint River, with a view to finding a good position (on the north bank if possible) for a battery for three or five guns and obstructions not to exceed 500 yards distant from the work. Heavier guns will be procured if possible.[11]

The final change to the orders stripped the proposed battery at Fort Gaines from all of its 32-pounders, leaving it with an 18-pounder and a 24-pounder. Hoping for better and larger guns at a future date, the Confederates started work on the installation in January of 1863. Lumber for the battery was sawed by David S. Johnston of Early County, the plantation owner who had built the gunboat CSS *Chattahoochee* at Saffold on the lower Chattahoochee River.

Emplacements for two pieces of artillery were dug down into the top of the bluff with the earth from the excavations being used to create protective earthworks and to cover magazines that would house ammunition for the guns. The 18-pounder and 24-pounder were mounted in these works and one of the pieces can still be seen there today. A third emplacement was later added at the bottom of the bluff, but little is known about the gun for which it was designed or even if one was ever mounted there.

The battery at Fort Gaines remained occupied by Confederate troops from January 1863 until the end of the war in April 1865. It never came under attack so its effectiveness was never tested. Had Union warships broken past the batteries and obstructions downstream on the Apalachicola, however, the guns at Fort Gaines would have provided the last-ditch defense for Columbus and its manufacturing facilities.

One of the three emplacements is still in excellent condition today and can be seen at the crest of the bluff near the site of the original fort. A dim trace of the second blufftop position is visible just to the south near the one-third scale reproduction of a blockhouse from the 1816 stockade. The height still provides a phenomenal view of the Chattahoochee River and the countryside for miles beyond.

Three Confederate military hospitals also operated at Fort Gaines in 1864, but were closed when the iron rails were removed from the Southwestern Railroad by order of the Southern government. These facilities provided treatment for wounded and sick soldiers from the Army of Tennessee. It is believed that Confederate wounded from the Battle of Olustee, Florida, were brought up the Chattahoochee to Fort Gaines by steamboat. The graves of men who did not survive their injuries or illnesses are at New Park Cemetery.

The end of the War Between the States signaled the end of Fort Gaines as a military post. The city is home to around 1,100 residents today and is a gateway to the beautiful Walter F. George Reservoir (Lake Eufaula) and Georgia's outstanding George T. Bagby State Park and Lodge. The landscape is dotted with historic landmarks, including the home of Elizabeth and John Dill, other antebellum and Victorian homes, the Sutton's Corner Museum, historic cemeteries and even a magnificent oak said to have been planted by Gen. Edmund P. Gaines.

---

[1] Charles Martin Gray, "The old soldier's story: autobiography of Charles Martin Gray, Co. A, 7th Regiment, U.S.I., embracing interesting and exciting incidents of army life on the frontier, in the early part of the present century," Edgefield Advertiser Print, 1868 – 63 pages.
[2] *Ibid.*
[3] *Arkansas Weekly Gazette*, April 7, 1821, p. 3.

[4] Samuel Forrey, M.D., late of the United States Army, Thomas Lawson, M.D., Surgeon General, Statistical Report on the Sickness and Mortality in the Army of the United States: Compiled from the Records of the Surgeon General's and Adjutant General's Offices – Embracing a Period of Twenty Years, from January, 1819, to January, 1839, Washington, printed by Jacob Gideon, Jr., 1840, p. 31.
[5] William P. Ford to Gov. William Schley, May 26, 1836.
[6] Col. John Dill to Gov. William Schley, May 27, 1836.
[7] Col. John Dill to Gov. William Schley, June 13, 1836.
[8] Maj. A.L. Rives to Capt. Theodore Moreno, November 18, 1862, *The War of the Rebellion*, Series 1, Volume XIV, p. 682.
[9] *Ibid.*
[10] Brig. Gen. Thomas Jordan to Brig. Gen. Howell Cobb, December 10, 1862, *The War of the Rebellion*, Series 1, Volume XIV, pp. 707-709.
[11] *Ibid.*

Photographs

Lt. Col. Duncan Lamont Clinch

Clinch as a brigadier general in later life.

Maj. Gen. Edmund Pendleton Gaines

Maj. Gen. Edmund P. Gaines by Matthew Brady

Restored blockhouse at Fort Gaines, Georgia.

Site of Fort Scott, Georgia.

Abraham, captured at destruction of the fort at Prospect Bluff.

Moat still surrounding the site of the fort at Prospect Bluff.

Brig. Gen. William McIntosh of Coweta.

Ben & Sam Perryman after the Trail of Tears.

The Prophet Josiah Francis (Self-Portrait).
Courtesy of the British Museum.

Neamathla (Eneah Emathla), chief of Fowltown.

Maj. David E. Twiggs, 7th U.S. Infantry Regiment.

Lt. Col. Matthew Arbuckle, 7th U.S. Infantry Regiment.

"Indians attacking Scott's party" (19th century sketch).

Site of the Scott Massacre of 1817 at River Landing Park in Chattahoochee, Florida.

Brig. Gen. WIlliam McIntosh

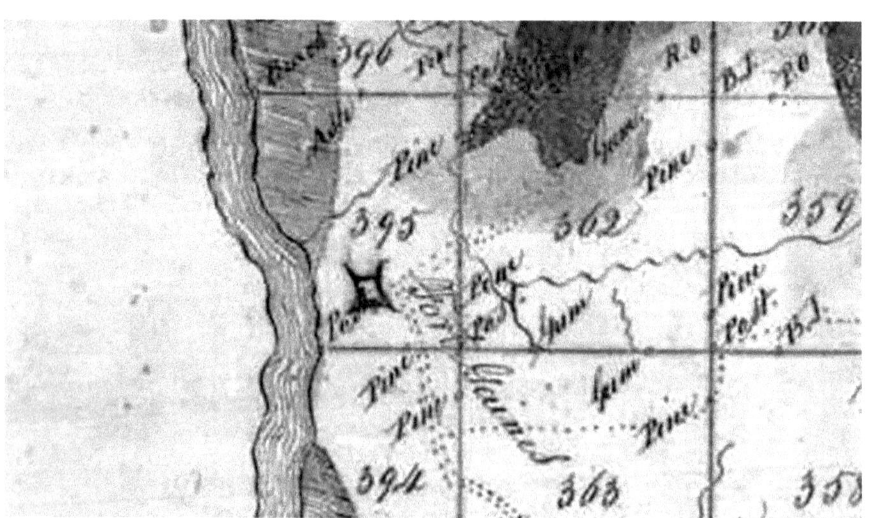

Fort Gaines in 1819

Grave of Elizabeth Dill in Fort Gaines, Georgia

Home of Elizabeth and John Dill in Fort Gaines, Georgia

References

Documents

Adams-Onis Treaty of 1819.

American State Papers, Foreign Relations, Volume IV, Washington, Gales and Seaton, 1834.

American State Papers, Indian Affairs, Volumes I & II. Washington, Gales and Seaton, 1834.

American State Papers, Military Affairs, Volume I, Washington, Gales and Seaton, 1834.

Army and Navy Chronicle, Volume 2 (New Series), 1836.

Andrew Jackson Papers, 1775-1874, Manuscript Reading Room, Library of Congress.

British Foreign and State Papers, Multiple Volumes, Her Majesty's Stationary Office.

Call Papers, State Archives of Florida.

District Plat of Survey for District 12, Early County (now Baker County), Georgia, 1819, State Archives of Georgia

District Plat of Survey for District 14, Early County (now Decatur County), Georgia, 1821, State Archives of Georgia.

Letters Received by the Adjutant General's Office during the period 1805-1821, M566, Record Group 94, National Archives, Washington, D.C.

Records of the Chief of Engineers, 1789-1996, Record Group 77, National Archives, Washington, D.C.

Register of Enlistments in the U.S. Army, 1798-1914, National Archives Microfilm Publication M233, 81 rolls, Records of the Adjutant General's Office, 1780's-1917, Record Group 94, National Archives, Washington, D.C.

Survey Book EEE, Office of the County Clerk, Decatur County, Georgia.
"The Indian Frontier in British East Florida: Letters to Governor James Grant from British Soldiers and Indian Traders," Florida History Online, University of North Florida, Online resource at www.unf.edu/floridahistoryonline/Projects/Grant/letters.html (transcribed by James Hill).
Territorial Papers of the United States: The Territory of Alabama, 1817-1819, Volume XVIII, Compiled and edited by Clarence Carter, Government Printing Office, Washington, D.C., 1952.
The War of the Rebellion: a Compilation of the Official Records of the Union and Confederate Armies, Series 1, Volume XIV, Government Printing Office, 1885.

Period Newspapers

Alexandria Gazette
American Beacon
Arkansas Gazette
Augusta Chronicle
Bainbridge Democrat
Baltimore Patriot
Camden Gazette
City Gazette
Easton Gazette
Georgia Journal
Hallowell Gazette
Independent American
London Times
Massachusetts Spy
Milledgeville Reflector
National Advocate
National Standard
Newburyport Herald
New York Daily Advertiser

New York Evening Post
New York Gazette
Niles Weekly Register
North Carolina Star
Spooner's Vermont Journal
Salem Gazette

Reports & Articles

Boyd, Mark F., "Historic Sites in and around the Jim Woodruff Reservoir Area, Florida-Georgia," River Basin Survey Papers, No. 13, *Bulletin 169*, Smithsonian Institution, Bureau of American Ethnology, 1958.

Forrey, Samuel, M.D., late of the United States Army, Thomas Lawson, M.D., Surgeon General, *Statistical Report on the Sickness and Mortality in the Army of the United States: Compiled from the Records of the Surgeon General's and Adjutant General's Offices – Embracing a Period of Twenty Years, from January, 1819, to January, 1839*, Washington, printed by Jacob Gideon, Jr., 1840

Doyle, Edmund, "Letters of Edmund Doyle," *Florida Historical Quarterly*, Volume 18, October 1939, No. 2.

Menefee, Samuel P., "Aaron Burr's Arrest," Encyclopedia of Alabama, online article at www.encyclopediaofalabama.org/article/h-2039, February 23, 2009.

Porter, Kenneth, "The Negro Abraham," *Florida Historical Quarterly*, Volume 25, July 1946.

Mark N. Schatz, "Reference Service Report: Monuments on the sites of Fort Scott, Fort Hughes, and Camp Recovery, near Bainbridge, Georgia," National Archives, 1953.

Suarez, Annette McDonald, "The War Path Across Georgia Made By Tennessee Troops in the First Seminole War," *The Georgia Historical Quarterly*, Vol. 38, No. 1, March 1954.

White, Nancy Marie, et. al., "Archaeology at Lake Seminole," Cleveland Museum of Natural History, 1980.

Books

Banks, John, *Diary of John Banks*, privately published, 1936.

Chapman, John Abney, *History of Edgefield County: from the earliest settlements to 1897: biographical and anecdotical, with sketches of the Seminole war, nullification, secession, reconstruction, churches and literature, with rolls of all the companies from Edgefield in the War of Secession, War with Mexico and with the Seminole Indians*, E.H. Aull, 1897.

Cox, Dale, *Fort Scott, Fort Hughes & Camp Recovery: Three 19th Century Military Sites in Southwest Georgia*, Old Kitchen Books, 2016.

Cox, Dale, *Milly Francis: The Life & Times of the Creek Pocahontas*, Old Kitchen Books, 2013.

Cox, Dale, *The Scott Massacre of 1817: A Seminole War Battle in Gadsden County, Florida*, West Gadsden Historical Society, 2013.

Cox, Dale, *Nicolls' Outpost: A War of 1812 Fort at Chattahoochee, Florida*, Old Kitchen Books, 2015.

Cox, Dale, *The Fort at Prospect Bluff*, scheduled for release in the winter of 2016-2017 by Old Kitchen Books.

Gray, Charles Martin, *The old soldier's story: autobiography of Charles Martin Gray, Co. A, 7th Regiment, U.S.I., embracing interesting and exciting incidents of army life on the frontier, in the early part of the present century*, Edgefield Advertiser Print.

Griffith, Benjamin W., Jr., *McIntosh and Weatherford: Creek Indian Leaders*, The University of Alabama Press, 1989.

Heitman, Francis Bernard, *Historical Register and Dictionary of the United States Army*, National Tribune Company, 1890.

Jones, Dixie May, and Mary Elizabeth Scott, *Citizens of Baldwin County, Mississippi Territory, in 1816 as enumerated in Inhabitants of Alabama in 1816*, Broken Arrow Chapter, Daughters of the American Revolution, 1955.

Missall, John and Mary Lou, *Elizabeth's War: A Novel of the First Seminole War*, The Florida Historical Society Press, 2015.

Woodward, Thomas Simpson, *Woodward's reminiscences of the Creek or Muscogee Indians: contained in letters to friends in Georgia and Alabama*, Montgomery, Alabama, 1859.

About the Author

Dale Cox is a writer and historian who lives near the quaint little community of Two Egg, Florida. He is the author of seventeen books on U.S. history.

Cox has written extensively about the history of Florida, Georgia, Alabama and Arkansas history from the era of Spanish exploration to the troubled times of the 1930s. His books have achieved critical acclaim and rank among the best-selling nonfiction books on history. He has been interviewed for hundreds of newspaper and magazine articles and will be featured next year on The Travel Channel.

His latest works include *Milly Francis: The Life & Times of the Creek Pocahontas*. The book covers the story of a young Creek Indian woman from her childhood in Alabama through the critical moment when she saved the life of a U.S. soldier during Florida's Seminole Wars.

The Battle of Marianna, Florida and *The Battle of Natural Bridge, Florida*, books by Cox about War Between the States battles in Florida, have been praised by critics as groundbreaking works on small Civil War engagements. Civil War Books & Authors called Cox "a skillful constructor of battle narrative."

Cox is a contributor to several tourism and heritage related websites:

- www.exploresouthernhistory.com
- www.battleofmarianna.com
- www.twoeggfla.com
- www.twoegg.tv

Active in historic preservation efforts and a popular speaker and story teller, Dale Cox was Jackson County's "Citizen of the Year" for 2012. He has been inducted into the prestigious Bonnie Blue Society for Southern writers and received the Judah P. Benjamin Award for his work in preserving the history of Florida. He was awarded the 2016 Golden Eagle award by the Boy Scouts of America.

A partner in the new "off the beaten path" tourism channel, Two Egg TV (www.twoegg.tv), Cox is a descendant of American frontiersman Daniel Boone.

Books by Dale Cox

Nicolls' Outpost: A War of 1812 fort at Chattahoochee, Florida
Death at Dozier School
Milly Francis: The Life & Times of the Creek Pocahontas
The Scott Massacre of 1817

The Claude Neal Lynching: The 1934 Murders of Claude Neal and Lola Cannady
The Ghost of Bellamy Bridge
The Battle of Natural Bridge, Florida
The Battle of Marianna, Florida
The Battle of Massard Prairie: The Confederate Attacks on Fort Smith, Arkansas
Old Parramore: The History of a Florida Ghost Town
The Early History of Gadsden County
The History of Jackson County, Florida: The Early Years
The History of Jackson County, Florida: The Civil War Years
Two Egg, Florida: A Collection of Ghost Stories, Legends & Unusual Facts
A Christmas in Two Egg, Florida: A Short Novel of Redemption
Fort Scott, Fort Hughes & Camp Recovery: Three 19th Century Military Sites in Southwest Georgia.
Fort Gaines, Georgia: A Military History

Index

1st U.S. Infantry, 17
4th U.S. Infantry, 13, 27, 43, *55*, ***65***, ***66***, ***70***, 107
7th U.S. Infantry, 63, ***65***, ***66***, ***70***, 102, 108
Abraham, 42
Alachua, 2
Ambrister
  Robert, 48
Amelia Island, ***70***, ***71***
Amelung
  Ferdinand Louis, 17
American Revolution, 50, 98
Apalachicola Bay, 35
Apalachicola River, 22, 26, 27, 30, 36, 42, 50, 64, ***69***
Arbuckle
  Lt. Col. Matthew, 106
  Matthew, 73, 75, 83, 91, 93
Arbuthnot
  Alexander, 48, *53*, *54*, 58, 104
Army of Tennessee, 135
Attapulgas, 99
Augusta Chronicle, 5
Aury
  Louis Michel. *See* Luis Aury
  Luis, ***71***
Autossee Mico, 99
Bahamas, 104
Bainbridge, 10, 22, 25
Baldwin County (Georgia), ***66***
Banks
  John, 115
Barnard
  Timothy, 26, *57*
Barnett. *See* Timothy Barnard
Barney, *54*
Bassett
  James, 40
Battle
  Econfina, 118
Battle of Econfina, 105, 114, 115, 116, 117, 120
Battle of Fowltown, 75
Battle of Hobdy's Bridge, 121
Battle of Horseshoe Bend, 24, 81, 99
Battle of New Orleans, 81
Battle of Ocheesee Bluff, 82
Battle of Olustee, 135
Battle of Prospect Bluff, 39
Battle of the Upper Chipola, 93
Bature, 42
Bay St. Louis, 42
Bear Head, 105
Beauregard
  P.G.T., 133
Big Warrior, 11, 13, 89
Black Seminoles, *53*, 111
Blackshear's Brigade, 65
Blood
  Young, 103
Bloody Bluff, 39
Blunt
  John, 23, 35, 37, 38
Boleck, 47, *52*, *53*, 94, 111, 112

Bolivar
  Simon, ***71***
Bowen
  Capt., 42
Bowlegs. *See* Boleck
Bowleg's Town. *See* Boleck
Bowles
  William Augustus, 50, 84
Brady
  Francis William, 93
Brearley
  David, 84, 85, 91
Breastworks (Early County), 74
Breastworks Branch, 74
Broken Arrow, 78
Buck
  Dr. Marcus, 40, 42
Burges
  James, 25
Burges's Bluff, 75
  Flint, 22
Burges's Old Place, 27
Burr
  Aaron, 3
Camden County (Georgia), 59
Camp Crawford, 33, 35, 41, 42, 58
  Flint, 31
Camp Montgomery, 11, 29, 43, 44, ***66***, ***67***, ***70***
Camp New Hope, 103
Camp Pinckney, 59
Cappachimico, *52*
Captain Isaacs, 36
Carney
  Miss Elizabeth, 104
Carter
  Jack, 116
Cemochechobee Creek, 4, 9
Chambers
  John, 76
Charles, 42, *54*
Charleston, 22, 27, 51, *56*, 59, 133
Chattahoochee River, 6, 15, 19, 25, 26, 29, 49, *56*, ***70***, 79
Chattahoochee Rivers, 22
Cherokee, 15
Chipola River, 84
Choctaw Chief, 37
Choctawhatchee River Blockhouse, ***67***
Choctaws, 26
Clark
  Archibald, *54*
Clinch
  Duncan Lamont, 3, 9, 19, 21, 27, 29, 31, 33, 35, 36, 37, 38, 41, 43, 47
Colonial Marines, 43, 48, *53*
Columbus, 132
Conecuh River, 65, ***70***
Cook
  Peter, 104, 106
Cordele, 78
County
  Clay, 118
  Early, 118
  Gadsden, *109*
  Jackson, 98, 103
  Leon, *109*
  Stewart, 130
Coweta, 42, 89, 103
  William, 11
Creek Brigade, 90
Creek Nation, 26, 121
Creek War of 1813-1814, 24, *54*, 89, 103, *See*
Creek War of 1836, 122
Creeks, 14, 15, 22, 23, 26, 35, ***68***, 76, 84
CSS Chattahoochee, 134
Culloh
  Alexander. *See* Alexander McCulloh
Cusseta, 130
Cutler

Enos, 11, 42, 84, 90
Dade
Maj. Francis, 107
Dade Massacre, 107
Dance of the Indians of the Lakes, 57
David S. Johnston, 134
Dexter
Horatio, 48
Dill
Elizabeth, 97
Elizabeth Stewart. *See* Elizabeth Stewart
John, 118, 121, 123, 130, 135
Dixie County (Florida), *53*
Donalsonville, 73
Donoho
Sanders, 59
Doyle
Edmund, 48, 59, ***67***
Duelling Bluff. *See* Bloody Bluff
Dulendo, 42
Early County, 10, 74, 127, 134
East Brewton, 7
East Florida, 47, ***71***
Econchattimico, 93
Ekanachatte, 93
Elijah, 42
Elizabeth Dill, 135
Eufaula, 90, 92, 131
Fernandina, ***71***
First Seminole War, 73, 86, 98, 103, 121
Flint River, 6, 15, 19, 24, 25, 27, 48, *56*, 57, ***68***, 78, 83
Flint Rivers, 22
Fort Apalachicola, 108
Fort at Prospect Bluff, 6, 16, 22, 23, 27, 28, 30, 31, 34, 38, 40, 42
Fort Claiborne, 4
Fort Crawford, 63, ***67***, 74
Fort Early, 78, 83
Fort Erie, 3
Fort Gadsden, 94, *109*, 127
Fort Gaines, 1, 10, 11, 17, 21, 23, 25, 26, 28, 29, 31, 33, 47, 50, *51*, *54*, *56*, 57, 58, 59, 63, ***67***, ***70***, 73, 74, 76, 77, 79, 82, 83, 84, 85, 86, 89, 90, 91, 92, 93, 94, 97, 118, 119, 120, 122, 127, 129, 130, 131, 133, 135
Fort Gaines Guards, 131
Fort Hawkins, 3, 6, 24, 44, *56*, ***66***, 78
Fort Hughes, 10, 76
Fort Jackson, 4, 14
Fort Mims, 3, 7, 29
Fort Mitchell, 3, 6, 43, 44, 78, 79, 80, 85, 90
Fort Montgomery, 7
Fort Perry, 85
Fort Scott, 31, 33, 44, 47, 48, 49, *56*, *57*, 59, 64, ***65***, ***67***, ***68***, 73, 74, 75, 76, 77, 80, 85, 86, 91, 100, 105, 127, 129
Fort Scott Road, 73
Fort Smith, 119
Fort St. Marks, 111, 112
Fort Stoddert, 3
Fort Strother, 4
Fort Twiggs, 130
Fort Williams, 4
Fowltown, *52*, ***68***, 74, 82, 90, 99
Francis
Josiah, 94, 99
Milly, 94
Gaines
Edmund P., 3, 5, 19, 24, 27, 28, 50, *55*, *56*, ***66***, ***67***, ***71***, 73, 76, 81
Edmund Pendleton, 4, 5, 9, 21, 74, 135
Maj. Gen. Edmund P., 101, 105
Gaines Oak, 135
Garrett Family, *53*
George T. Bagby State Park, 135

Glasscock
Thomas, 78
Graham
George, 48, ***67***, ***70***, 82
Gray
Charles Martin, 127, 128
Survivor, Scott Massacre, 100, 102, 103, 108
Gulf Power Company, 98
Hambly
William, 26, 30, 59
Hamilton's Brigade, 65
Hancock County (Georgia), ***66***
Hardridge
William, 25
Hartford, 25, 65
Hawkins
Benjamin, 14, 19, 21, 23, 27, 42, *55*
Hayne
A.P., 85
Homathlemico, 99, 111
Howell
W.B., 42
Hughes
Aaron, 75
Indian Removal Act, 120
Infantry
4th U.S., 3
Iron City, 73
Irvin
Robert, 80
Irwin's Brigade, 65
Irwinton. See Eufaula
Jackson
Andrew, 4, 19, 24, 27, 31, *55*, *56*, ***65***, ***68***, ***70***, 76, 81, 85, 86
Maj. Gen. Andrew, 100, *110*, 112, 120
Jackson County (Florida), 84
Jacob, 42
Jamaica, 41, 42
James
William, 108
Jasper County (Georgia), ***66***
Jefferson
Thomas, 120
Jo, 42
Joe, *54*
John Dill House, 119
John Forbes & Company, 48, ***67***
Johnson
Daniel, 3
Johnson & McGaskey Murders, 5, 14, 31
Jones County (Georgia), ***66***
Jordan
Thomas, 133
Kenard
Maj. Noble. *See* Noble Kinnard
Kenhajo. *See* Cappachimico
King
William, 43, 44, *55*
Kingsley
Zephaniah, 47, 49
Kinnard
Maj. Noble, 113, 115, 120
Kolomoki Creek, 127
Lafarka. *See* John Blunt
Lake Eufaula, 135
Lake Miccosukee, 104
Lamb, 42
Lewis
Kendal, 36
Mr., 42
Little Prince, 11, 13, 15, 17, 23, 26, 27, 78
Little River, 23
Loomis
Jairus, 36, 39
Lower Creeks, 17, *54*, ***69***, 78
Lumpkin, 130
Gov. Wilson, 121
MacGregor
Gregor, ***71***
Mad Tiger, 36

Margart
  William, 42
McCrimmon
  Duncan, 94
McCulloh
  Alexander, 58
McHenry
  James. *See* Jim Henry
McIntosh
  Brig. Gen. William, 101, 103, 112, 113, 115, 117
  Sgt. Frederick, 102, 103
  William, 11, 21, 35, 36, 38, 42, *57*, 58, 80, 84, 89, 90, 92
McKeever
  Lt. Isaac, 112
McQueen
  Peter, 24, *54*, *55*, 99, 111, 113
Miccosukee, 2, 26, 49, *54*, ***68***, 79, 94, 99, 111, 112
Mico de Coxe, 84
Milledgeville, 34, 47, 50, ***66***
Mississippi River, 17
Mitchell
  David B., 48, 50, *51*, 57, 78, 81, 117
  William, 117
Mobile, 99
Moreno
  Theodore, 132
Morgan County (Georgia), ***66***
Muhlenberg
  Peter, 36, 42
Muhlenburg
  Maj. Peter, 104, 108
Mulatto King, 98, 103
Murder Creek, 7
Natural Bridge of the Econfina, 111, 112, 113
Natural Well Branch, 111
Neamathla, 74, 75, 122
Negro Fort, 4, 14, 15, 33, 94, *See* Fort at Prospect Bluff
Nero, 94
New Oleans, 85
New Orleans, 28, 30
New Park Cemetery, 135
Newspaper
  Augusta Chronicle, 78
  Georgia Journal, ***66***
Nicolls
  Edward, 4, 24, 43, 47, 48, *52*, *55*, 99
Ochlockonee River, *54*, *56*
Ochlockonee Sound, *54*, 59
Oketeyocanne, 25
Old Pioneer Cemetery, 10
Old Town, *53*
Onis Hadjo, 80, 91
Osceola, 111
Osoochie, 79
Patriot Revolt, 103
Payne, *52*
Pensacola, 16, 17, 41, 43, *51*, ***67***, 94
Perry, 110
Perryman
  Ben, 50
  George, 44, 49, 50, *51*, *53*, *56*
  Theophilus, 50
  Thomas, 50
  William, 50, *55*
Perryman's Old Town, 73
Peter McQueen, 105
Pioneer Cemetery
  Fort Gaines, Georgia, 123
Point Petre, ***70***
Powell
  Billy, 111
Prospect Bluff, 4, 15, 21, 25, 29, 38, 39, 43, 48, *52*, *53*, ***67***
Pulaski County (Georgia), ***66***
Putnam County (Georgia), ***66***
Rabun
  William, ***66***
Red Ground, 93

Red Sticks, 4, 24, 27, 48, 50, *51*, *53*, *54*, 57, 64, ***69***, 79, 100, *110*
Regiment
4th Infantry, 9
4th U.S. Infantry, 73
7th Infantry, 129
7th U.S. Infantry, 73, 127
Republic of Mexico, ***71***
River
Alabama, 11, 97
Apalachicola, 4, 23, 97, 100, 103, 129
Arkansas, 129
Chattahoochee, 1, 7, 9, 21, 73, 89, 121
Choctawhatchee, 63
Econfina, 114
Flint, 10, 22, 31, 91
Ochlockonee, *109*
Red, 129
St. Marks, 112
St. Mary's, 105
Suwannee, 94, 104, 111
Tallapoosa, 3
Yellow Water, 63
Rives
A.L., 132
Roanoke, 130, 131
Roanoke Massacre, 130
Rock Bluff, 133
Saffold, 134
San Marcos de Apalache, 94
Sands
Richard M., 50, *51*, *55*, *56*, 58, ***67***
Schley
Gov. William, 122, 130
Scott
Lt. Richard W., 100, 101, 106
Richard W., 78, 97
Scott Massacre, 92, 97
Scott Massacre of 1817, 81
Scott's Brigade, 65
Second Seminole War, 107
Seminole County, 73
Seminoles, 2, 14, 22, 24, 25, 26, 27, 37, 42, 48, *53*, *55*, 64, ***68***, ***69***, 79, 81
Ship
General Pike, 41
Gunboat #149, 39
Gunboat #154, 40
Sea Horse, 43
Semelante, 39
Smith
Col. Thomas A., 102, 103
St. Augustine, 41, 48
St. Johns River, 49
St. Marks, 24, 94, 112, 113
St. Marys, *54*, 59, 81
St. Marys River, 59, 76
St. Stephens, ***66***
Stewart
Elizabeth, 101, 104, 108, *110*, 111, 113, 114, 119, 123, 131
Sutton's Corner Museum, 135
Suwannee River, 48, *52*, ***69***
Suwannee River Water Management District, 111
Tallahassee, 110
Tallahassee Talofa, 94, *109*, 113
Tame King, 92
Tate's Hell Swamp, *109*
Taylor
William, 36
Tharp
John, 42
The Narrows, 133
Thomas Shields
Warship, 112
Three Notch Road, 73, 74
Timbora, 97
Touson (Towson)
James, 123
Sarah, 123
Treaty of Fort Jackson, 1, 3, 11, 21, ***68***

Troup
  George, 89
Tuckabatchee, *54*
Twiggs
  David E., 7, 63, ***67***, ***69***, 74, 128
  Maj. David E., *110*, 113
Twiggs County (Georgia), ***66***
Underground Railroad, 4
Walker
  Joel, 10
Walter F. George Reservoir, 135
War of 1812, 24, 50, *55*, 63, ***69***
Wash
  Richard, 127
Washington County (Georgia), ***66***
Washington, D.C., 81
Wayne County (Georgia), 50, *53*, 59
Wellborn
  William, 121
West Florida, ***71***
Wetumpka, 14
William, 42
Woodbine
  George, 47, 48, *52*
Woodward
  Maj. Thomas, 101, 102, 108, 115, 117
  Thomas, 77
Wright
  Maj. Clinton, 104, 108
Yellow Hair, 98, 103, 105
Yellow Water River, ***70***
Yellow Water River Blockhouse, ***67***
Yuchi, 57, 90
Yuchi Billy, 99
Yuchi Old Fields, 90
Zuniga
  Mauricio de, 15, 31

www.ingramcontent.com/pod-product-compliance
Lightning Source LLC
Chambersburg PA
CBHW071052040426
42443CB00013B/3316